EXPLORING TRADITIONAL SCALES AND CHORDS FOR JAZZ KEYBOARD

by Bill Boyd

INTRODUCTION

Scales and chord tones provide the basis for jazz improvisation and fill-ins. This book explores the scales and chords within the framework of a chord progression and examines their potential. While this is not a jazz improvisation method, the study of the material will certainly provide the player with additional resources in this area.

The scale chapters include charts with the scales written in all keys and the chords which complement each scale written underneath. Music examples apply the scales and chord tones to jazz chord progressions.

A knowledge of scale and chord construction is helpful to fully benefit from the material presented. Upon completion of this volume, the keyboard player will gain new insights into the practical application of scales and chord tones to jazz chord progressions and compositions and enhance performance.

ISBN 978-0-7935-6168-1

HAL•LEONARD®
CORPORATION

7777 W. BLUEMOUND RD. P.O. BOX 13819 MILWAUKEE, WI 53213

1: THE FUNCTION OF CHORDS

The scales and chords presented in this book provide the basis for improvised jazz lines or short fill-ins and endings. In order to determine which scale is appropriate for a particular chord, it is necessary to know where the chord appears within the context of a chord progression. In other words, realize how the chord FUNCTIONS within the chord progression.

The function of chords is best described in terms of Roman numerals. The scale tones in a given key are numbered from one to seven. The first note of a scale is called the TONIC (or 1). It is the note for which the scale is named.

C Major Scale:

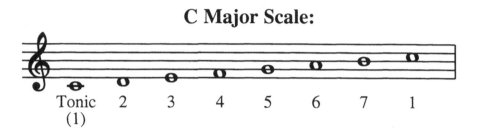

Chords constructed on these scale tones are labeled with Roman numerals which correspond to the scale steps. The note in the scale upon which the chord is constructed is called the chord ROOT. The letter name of the chord is the same as the chord root.

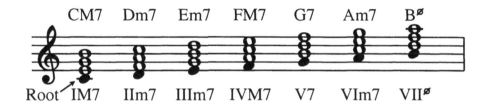

The chord type (major, minor, dominant 7th) at any level may vary. The F major seventh chord in the last example could be a dominant seventh or minor seventh, etc.

To select a scale which would complement a Dm7 chord, it is necessary to determine the function of the chord within the context of a chord progression. For example, the Dm7 chord functions as a II chord in the key of C, a VI chord in the key of F and a III chord in the key of B♭.

Each function of the Dm7 chord will require a different scale for improvisation. The scale which complements a Dm7 chord in the key of C will not work with the Dm7 chord in the key of F.

It is necessary to convert the letter-name chord symbols to Roman numerals to determine the function of a particular chord. Many jazz tunes change keys within the composition. Key changes are established by the presence of the V7-I or IIm7-V7-I chord progressions. The I chord, which is some type of major chord in a major key, is called the TONIC or KEY chord. Not all major chords are tonic chords but if they are preceded by the IIm7-V7, a new key is established. The I chord in a minor key is some type of minor chord. When a key change occurs the Roman numerals must be adjusted in terms of the new key. The following example is in the key of C major, but the key changes within the eight measure section.

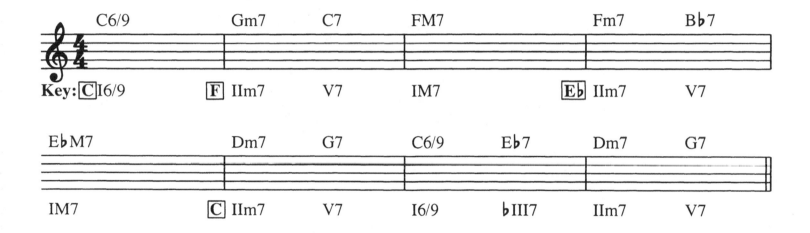

Sometimes just the presence of a V7 or a IIm7-V7 is enough to establish a new key momentarily. This situation is more difficult to analyze because the key chord is not present. Therefore, it is important to recognize the II-V-I progression in all major and minor keys. Study the chart below.

MAJOR KEYS

KEY	IIm7	V7	I
C	Dm7	G7	C
Db	Ebm7	Ab7	Db
D	Em7	A7	D
Eb	Fm7	Bb7	Eb
E	F#m7	B7	E
F	Gm7	C7	F
Gb	Abm7	Db7	Gb
G	Am7	D7	G
Ab	Bbm7	Eb7	Ab
A	Bm7	E7	A
Bb	Cm7	F7	Bb
B	C#m7	F#7	B

In minor keys the letter names of the three chords are the same. However, the II chord is m7♭5 and the I chord is some type of minor chord.

MINOR KEYS

Key	IIm7♭5	V7	Im
Cm	Dm7♭5	G7	Cm
D♭m	E♭m7♭5	A♭7	D♭m
Dm	Em7♭5	A7	Dm
E♭m	Fm7♭5	B♭7	E♭m
Em	F♯m7♭5	B7	Em
Fm	Gm7♭5	C7	Fm
G♭m	A♭m7♭5	D♭7	G♭m
Gm	Am7♭5	D7	Gm
A♭m	B♭m7♭5	E♭7	A♭m
Am	Bm7♭5	E7	Am
B♭m	Cm7♭5	F7	B♭m
Bm	C♯m7♭5	F♯7	Bm

MUSIC EXAMPLES

The music examples are not meant to be jazz improvisations as such. They illustrate the subject matter of a particular chapter. For example, the scales often appear in their entirety so the player will be able to hear all of the notes as they relate to the chord. In practical playing situations sometimes only a portion of the scale is applied to an improvisation and is often combined with chord tones, pentatonic and blues scales.

All examples are notated with no key signatures. All accidentals are written in. The chord symbols appear over the staff and the Roman numerals, when pertinent, are written under the staff.

It is helpful to have some knowledge of scale and chord construction in order to fully benefit from the material presented.

2: THE MAJOR SCALE

C Major Scale

The major scale will complement the following chord types.

    6   6/9   M7   M7$\sharp$11

    m7   m9   m11

    Dominant 7th   9th   13th   suspended

    RESTRICTIONS: Not to be played with altered dominant sevenths or V7 in minor keys.

The major scales in all keys appear at the end of this chapter. The chords which complement each scale are written underneath.

The chord progession IM7-VIm7-IIm7-V7 is most common. The major scale which has the same letter name as the I chord will complement all chords in this progression.

        Key of C major:

            CM7   Am7   Dm7   G7

            IM7   VIm7   IIm7   V7

The C major scale will complement this progression.

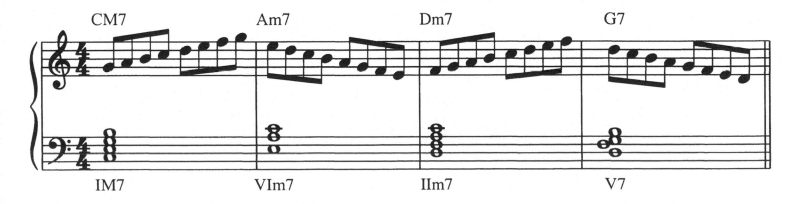

It is often best not to play any scale from tonic to tonic. Scales may start and end on any note and proceed in any direction. It is not necessary to include all scale tones in every melodic idea.

As with all scales presented in this book, there are some notes which do not fit the chord as well as others. The 4th scale step is sometimes avoided on the I chord. Measure one of the preceding example contains the 4th (F) with the I chord. Notice that it is perfectly acceptable when it is passed through quickly. It is helpful to practice the major scales without the 4th for use with the I chord. The C, G, F and B♭ major scales appear below without the 4th.

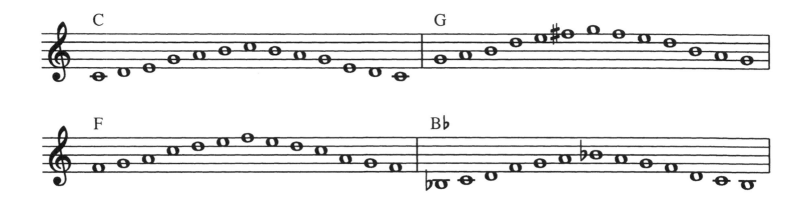

The following example is an ending in the key of B♭ major. The B♭ major scale without the 4th is played with the I chord.

Certain devices may be applied to any scale to provide variety.

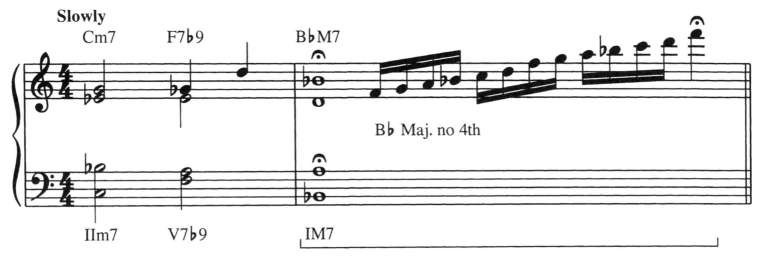

Fourths:

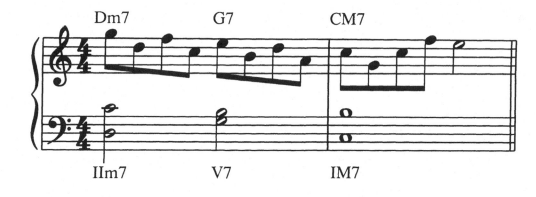

Skips: Skips may occur at any point.

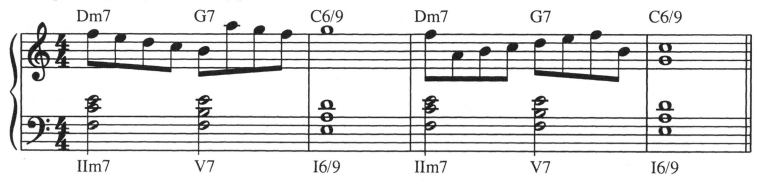

Sequence: A note pattern is repeated at various levels of the scale.

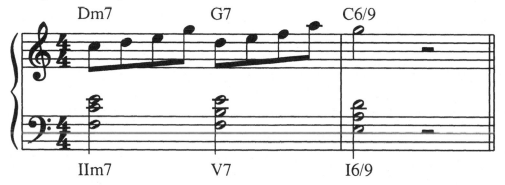

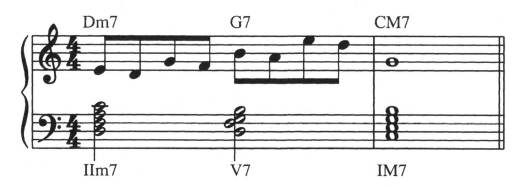

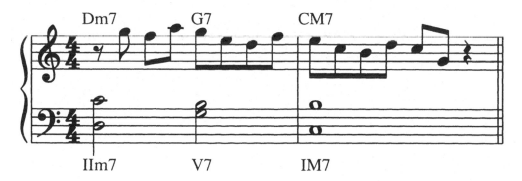

The major scale which has the same letter name as the I chord will complement the IIIm7 chord. In the key of C major the C major scale is played with the IIIm7 chord. In this instance the IIIm7 is treated as a substitute for the I chord.

The major scale which has the same letter name as the I chord will complement the IVM7 chord. In the following example the C major scale is applied to the FM7 chord.

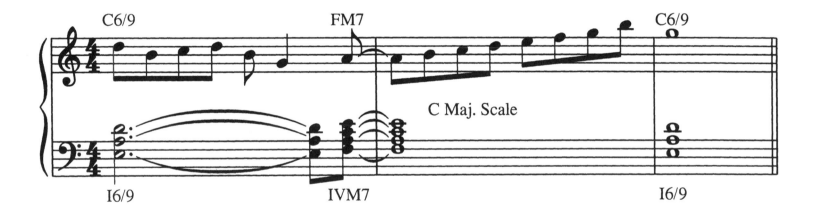

SUMMARY:

The C major scale will complement the following chords:

The chord function must always be considered. Each chord in the example above could be complemented by a different scale if the function were changed.

The next example illustrates the major scale as a fill-in on a slow ballad. The D♭ major scale is played with the E♭m7 chord. The chord moves to an A♭7 in the next measure. This progression is treated as a temporary II-V in the key of D♭ and the scale of the I chord is selected. The I chord does not appear. Therefore it is most important to know and recognize the II-V-I chord progression in all keys in order to select the proper scale. (See Chapter 1.)

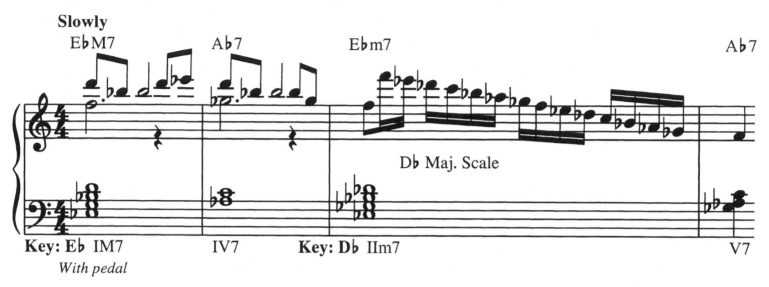

The following improvisation is a series of chromatic dominant seventh chords. Each chord is treated as the V7 chord of a major key. The major scale which has the same letter name as the I chord is selected. In measure one, the B♭ major scale complements the F9 chord. From this point on, all of the examples in this book will indicate the scale choice in the middle of the staff.

Another series of chromatic dominant seventh chords follows. In this instance each dominant seventh chord is preceded by a minor 7th chord to establish a temporary II-V relationship.

The following exercise is a series of IIm7-V7-I chord progressions in several keys. Notice how the scales are linked together to form a smooth melodic line.

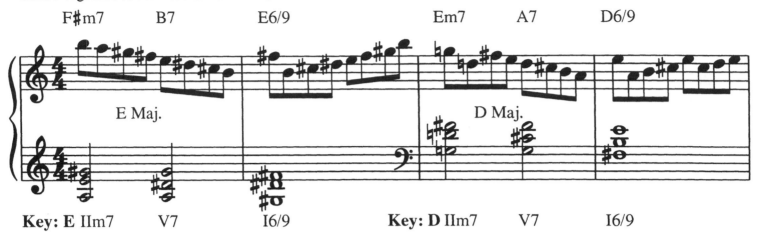

The next improvisation is the same chord progression with various rhythm patterns.

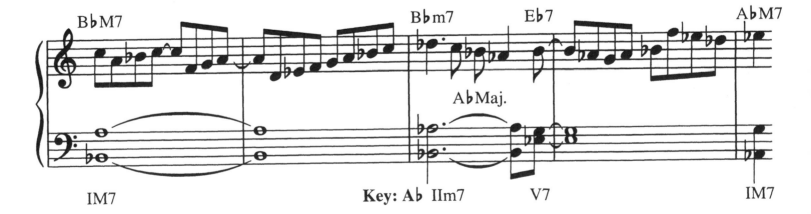

Below is a series of dominant seventh chords. Each chord is treated as if it were a V7 chord of a major key. In measure one the C7 chord is the V7 chord in the key of F major. The F major scale is selected for this chord.

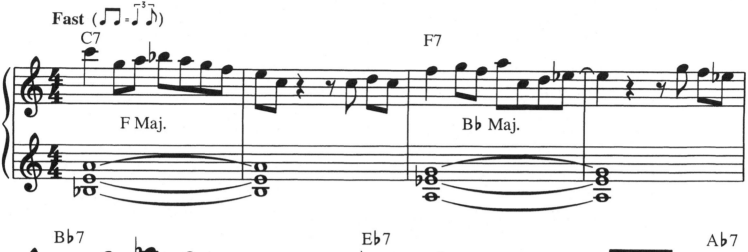

The 6/9 chord is accompanied by the major scale which has the same name as the chord root regardless of function.

For dominant 7th suspended chords play the major scale without the fourth whose tonic is one whole step below, the chord root. In the example below, the Bb major scale (without the 4th) is played with the C7sus.

Throughout this book the scale choice will often depend upon which notes of the chord are to be emphasized. In the example below the G major scale is played with the CM7#11 chord to emphasize the #11. The Ab major scale is played with the DbM7#11. This example could be played as an ending.

For any M7#11 chord, play the major scale constructed on the note a perfect 5th above the chord root regardless of function.

Another example of the M7#11 chord follows:

The melody below has several pauses where fill-ins may be inserted.

The same melody with fill-ins:

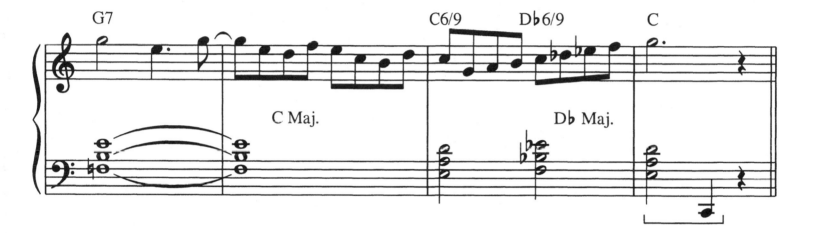

Below is a chord/scale relationship chart. The C chords serve as examples. Chord/scale relationships in any key may be found by transposing the chart.

SUMMARY

Chord	Function	Major Scale
C6/9	any	C
CM7	I	C
CM7	IV	G
CM7♯11	any	G
Cm7 9 11	II	B♭
Cm7	III	A♭
Cm7	VI	E♭
C7 9 13	any except V7 minor key	F
C7sus	V	B♭ no 4th

MAJOR SCALES

C

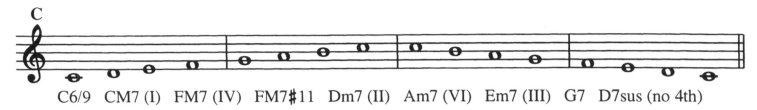

C6/9   CM7 (I)   FM7 (IV)   FM7#11   Dm7 (II)   Am7 (VI)   Em7 (III)   G7   D7sus (no 4th)

Db

Db6/9   DbM7 (I)   GbM7 (IV)   GbM7#11   Ebm7 (II)   Bbm7 (VI)   Fm7 (III)   Ab7   Eb7sus (no 4th)

D

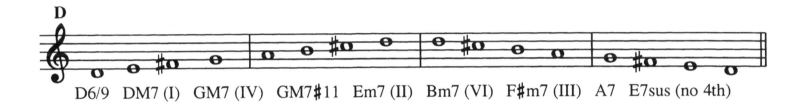

D6/9   DM7 (I)   GM7 (IV)   GM7#11   Em7 (II)   Bm7 (VI)   F#m7 (III)   A7   E7sus (no 4th)

Eb

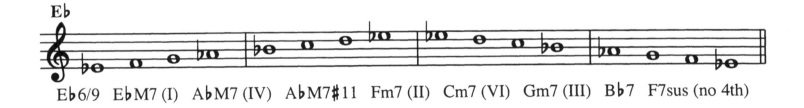

Eb6/9   EbM7 (I)   AbM7 (IV)   AbM7#11   Fm7 (II)   Cm7 (VI)   Gm7 (III)   Bb7   F7sus (no 4th)

E

E6/9   EM7 (I)   AM7 (IV)   AM7#11   F#m7 (II)   C#m7 (VI)   G#m7 (III)   B7   F#7sus (no 4th)

F

F6/9   FM7 (I)   BbM7 (IV)   BbM7#11   Gm7 (II)   Dm7 (VI)   Am7 (III)   C7   G7sus (no 4th)

15

Gb

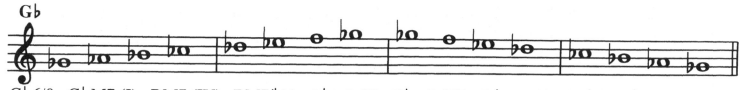

Gb6/9   GbM7 (I)   BM7 (IV)   BM7#11   Abm7 (II)   Ebm7 (VI)   Bbm7 (III)   Db7   Ab7sus (no 4th)

G

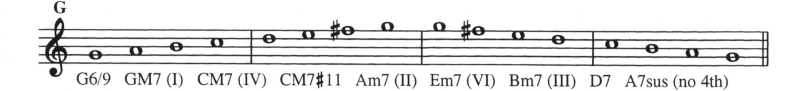

G6/9   GM7 (I)   CM7 (IV)   CM7#11   Am7 (II)   Em7 (VI)   Bm7 (III)   D7   A7sus (no 4th)

Ab

Ab6/9   AbM7 (I)   DbM7 (IV)   DbM7#11   Bbm7 (II)   Fm7 (VI)   Cm7 (III)   Eb7 Bb7sus (no 4th)

A

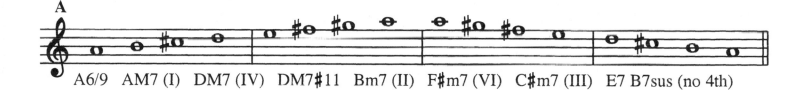

A6/9   AM7 (I)   DM7 (IV)   DM7#11   Bm7 (II)   F#m7 (VI)   C#m7 (III)   E7 B7sus (no 4th)

Bb

Bb6/9   BbM7 (I)   EbM7 (IV)   EbM7#11 Cm7 (II)   Gm7 (VI)   Dm7 (III)   F7 C7sus (no 4th)

B

B6/9   BM7 (I)   EM7 (IV)   EM7#11 C#m7 (II)   G#m7 (VI)   D#m7 (III)   F#7 C#7sus (no 4th)

3: THE (NATURAL) MINOR SCALE

C Minor Scale:

The minor scale will complement the following chord types:

m (triad)
m6
m7♭5 (∅)
dom. 7th ♯5 ♭9 ♯9

RESTRICTIONS: Does not fit m6 functioning as a I.

The minor scales in all keys appear at the end of this chapter. The chords which complement each scale are written underneath.

In a minor key, the II chord is a m7♭5. The V chord is an altered dominant seventh. The chord progression Im-IIm7♭5-V7 may be complemented by the minor scale which has the same letter name as the I chord.

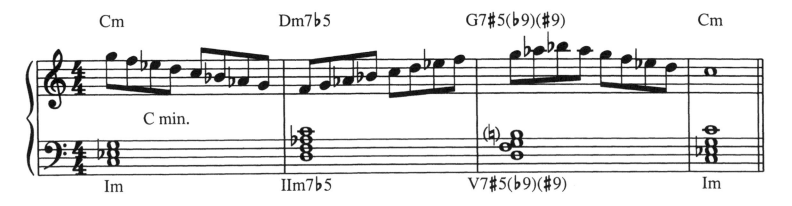

The minor scale emphasizes the ♯5 ♭9 and ♯9 in the dominant 7th chord. The chord symbol is sometimes written G7 alt. instead of listing the many altered notes.

Notice the use of thirds and sequence in the following example.

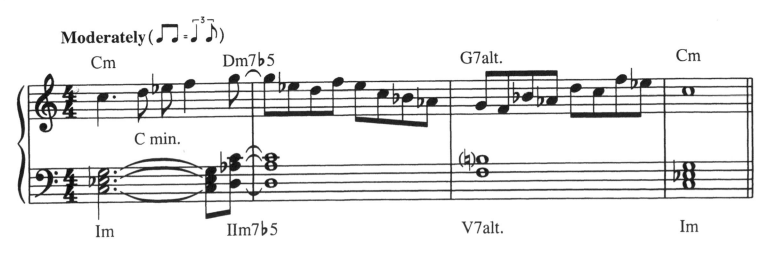

Another example in the key of D minor follows.

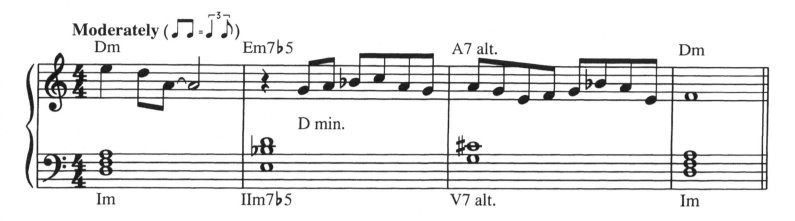

When a m6 chord functions as a IV (not a I) in a major or minor key, play the minor scale which has the same letter name as the I chord.

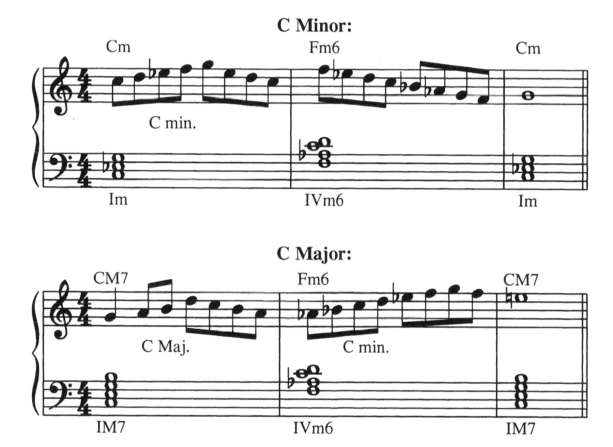

The next example illustrates a fill-in on a minor 6th chord in the key of C major.

The m7♭5 chord is sometimes called a half diminished 7th chord.

Chord symbol: ∅

The m7♭5 contains the same notes as a m6 chord.

To select a scale for any m7♭5 chord regardless of function, think of the chord as a IIm7♭5 in a minor key. Choose the minor scale which has the same letter name as the I chord. (Ex. Cm7♭5 play B♭m.)

The minor scale emphasizes the ♯5 ♭9 and ♯9 in a dominant 7th chord functioning as a V7 in a major key. The next example is in the key of C major.

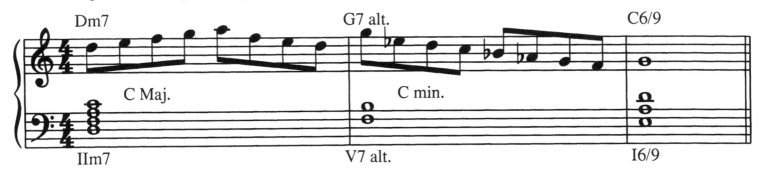

SUMMARY

Chord	Function	Minor Scale
Cm (triad)	I	C
Cm6	IV	G
Cm7♭5 C∅	any	B♭
C7♯5(♭9)(♯9)	V	F

PLAYING FROM A FAKE BOOK

Upon completion of each chapter, select tunes from a fake book and apply the scales as fill-ins, endings or improvisations. Fake books do not always indicate four note chords. Major triads should be played as major 7th or 6/9 and minor chords are changed to m7. Dominant 7th chords may or may not be altered. Analyze the chords in terms of their function. Look for key changes. Adjust the Roman numerals in terms of the new key. Look on the scale charts at the end of the chapters to see which scales complement a particular chord. A chord/scale relationship chart listing all chord types and all scales appears on page 54.

(NATURAL) MINOR SCALES

Cm

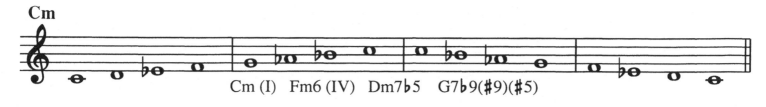

Cm (I)   Fm6 (IV)   Dm7b5   G7b9(#9)(#5)

Dbm
C#m

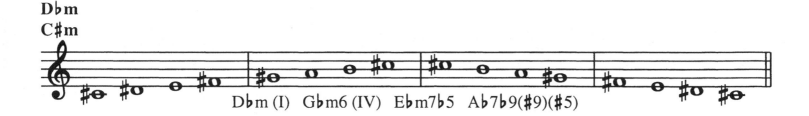

Dbm (I)   Gbm6 (IV)   Ebm7b5   Ab7b9(#9)(#5)

Dm

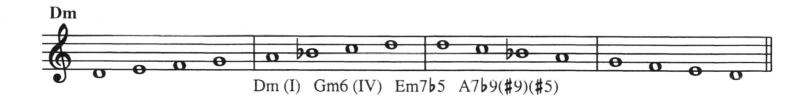

Dm (I)   Gm6 (IV)   Em7b5   A7b9(#9)(#5)

Ebm

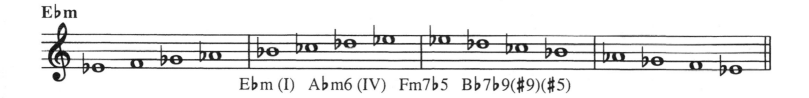

Ebm (I)   Abm6 (IV)   Fm7b5   Bb7b9(#9)(#5)

Em

Em (I)   Am6 (IV)   F#m7b5   B7b9(#9)(#5)

Fm

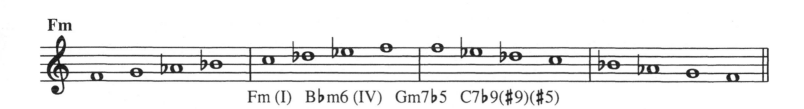

Fm (I)   Bbm6 (IV)   Gm7b5   C7b9(#9)(#5)

F#m
Gbm

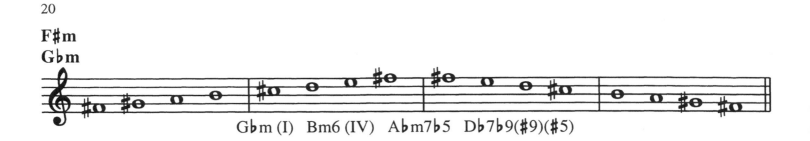

Gbm (I)   Bm6 (IV)   Abm7b5   Db7b9(#9)(#5)

Gm

Gm (I)   Cm6 (IV)   Am7b5   D7b9(#9)(#5)

G#m
Abm

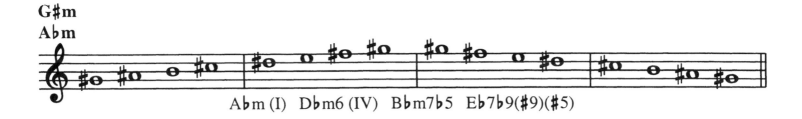

Abm (I)   Dbm6 (IV)   Bbm7b5   Eb7b9(#9)(#5)

Am

Am (I)   Dm6 (IV)   Bm7b5   E7b9(#9)(#5)

Bbm

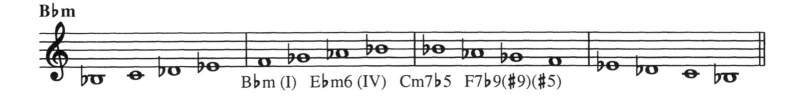

Bbm (I)   Ebm6 (IV)   Cm7b5   F7b9(#9)(#5)

Bm

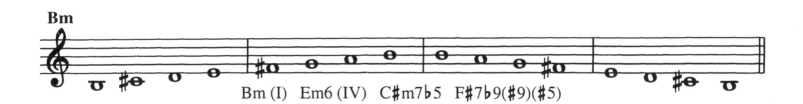

Bm (I)   Em6 (IV)   C#m7b5   F#7b9(#9)(#5)

4: THE HARMONIC MINOR SCALE

C Harmonic Minor Scale:

The harmonic minor scale will complement the following chord types:

    m (triad)

    m(maj7)

    dom. 7th ♯5 ♭9

The harmonic minor scales in all keys appear at the end of this chapter. The chords which complement each scale are written underneath.

The harmonic minor scale may be played with the V7 and I chords in minor keys. The IIm7♭5 chord is complemented by the minor scale.

Another example of II-V-I in the key of C minor:

The harmonic minor scale will emphasize the ♭9 (along with the ♯5) in a dominant seventh chord regardless of function. The next example is a V7♭9 in the key of C major.

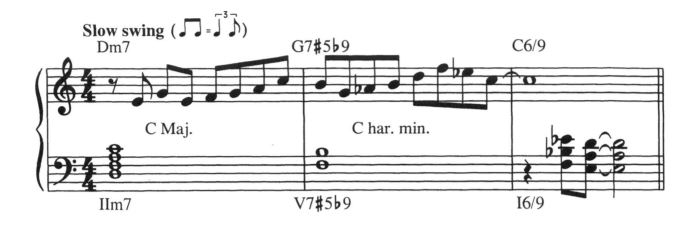

Often improvisations on the III7, VI7 and VII7 chords in a major key will emphasize the ♯5 and the ♭9 even though the chord symbol indicates a dominant 7th with no alterations. To select the appropriate scale, treat each dominant seventh chord as a V7 in a minor key. Choose the harmonic minor scale which has the same letter name as the I chord in the minor key.

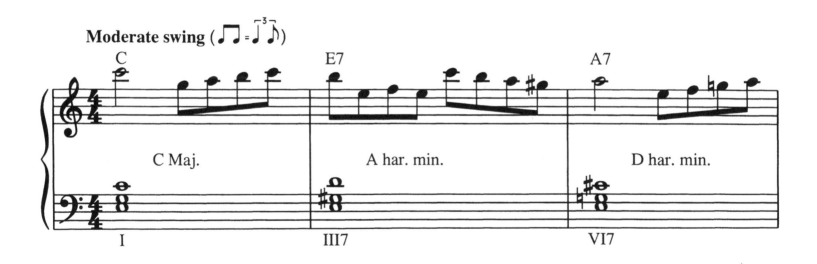

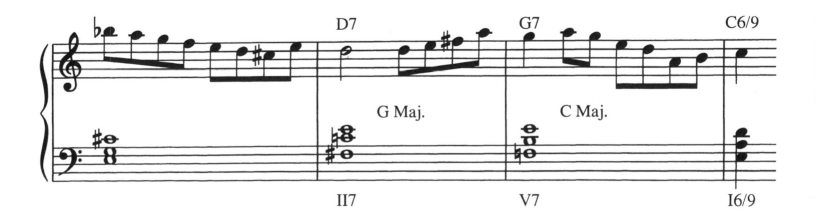

The next exercise presents a very common treatment of the VI7♭9 chord in a major key.

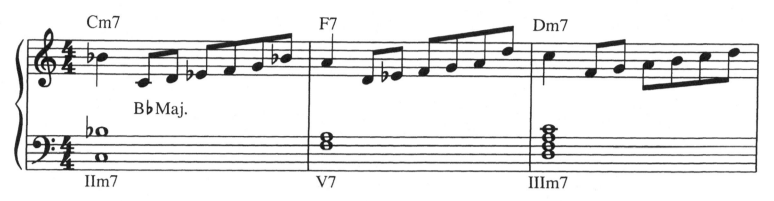

Sometimes in the above example the IIIm7 (Dm7) is a IIIm7♭5. In this instance the Dm7♭5-G7♭9 are treated as a temporary key change to Cm. The Dm7♭5 takes the Cm scale and the G7♭9 takes the C harmonic minor scale. The next exercise illustrates this situation in measures three and four. The key is E♭ major and the Gm7 chord could be analyzed as a III chord.

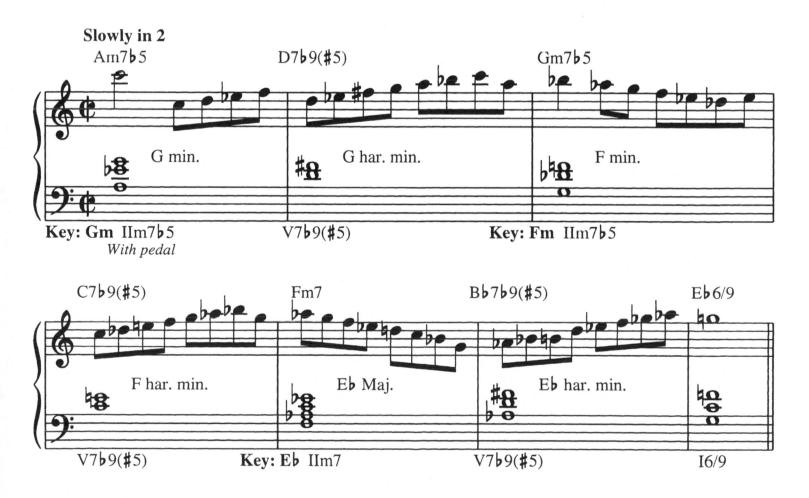

The minor chord with the major 7th added is complemented by the harmonic minor scale which has the same letter name as the chord root. It appears most often as a I chord.

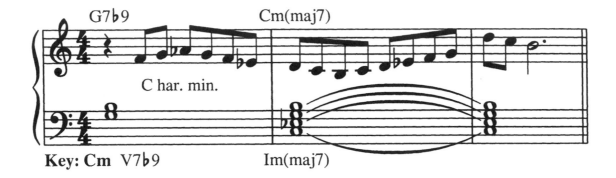

When the chords change every two beats not all scale tones are present.

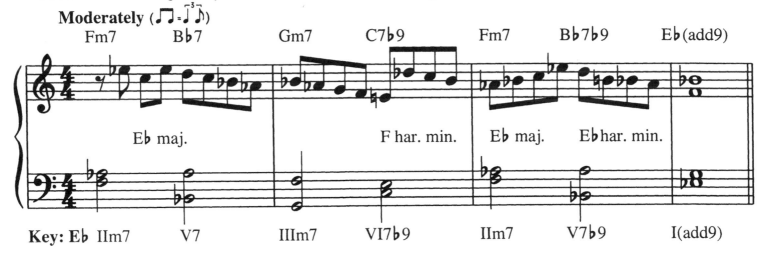

SUMMARY

Chord	Function	Harmonic Minor Scale
Cm (triad)	I	C
Cm(maj7)	I (any)	C
C7♯5(♭9)	any	F

As you proceed through this book you will notice that there are often several scale choices for the same chord type. In Chapter 3 the minor scale complemented the V7♯5(♭9)(♯9) chord. In this chapter the harmonic minor scale is applied to the V7♯5(♭9) chord. The scale choice always depends upon which notes of the chord you wish to emphasize and which scale sounds best in a given situation.

HARMONIC MINOR SCALES

Cm (I) Cm(maj7) G7♭9(♯5)

D♭m (I) D♭m(maj7) A♭7♭9(♯5)

Dm (I) Dm(maj7) A7♭9(♯5)

E♭m (I) E♭m(maj7) B♭7♭9(♯5)

Em (I) Em(maj7) B7♭9(♯5)

Fm (I) Fm(maj7) C7♭9(♯5)

26

F♯m
G♭m

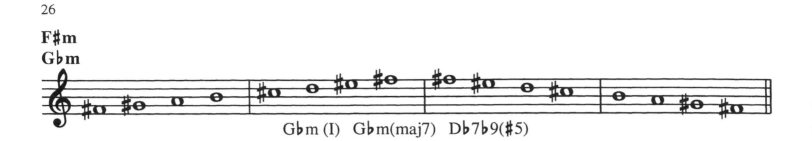

Gbm (I)   Gbm(maj7)   Db7b9(#5)

Gm

Gm (I)   Gm(maj7)   D7b9(#5)

G♯m
A♭m

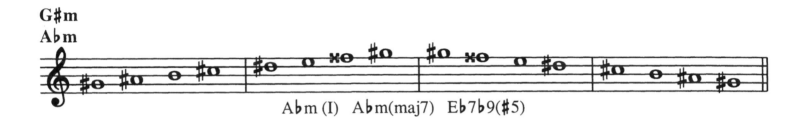

Abm (I)   Abm(maj7)   Eb7b9(#5)

Am

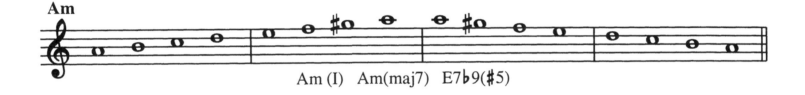

Am (I)   Am(maj7)   E7b9(#5)

B♭m

Bbm (I)   Bbm(maj7)   F7b9(#5)

Bm

Bm (I)   Bm(maj7)   F#7b9(#5)

5: THE HARMONIC MAJOR SCALE

C Harmonic Major Scale:

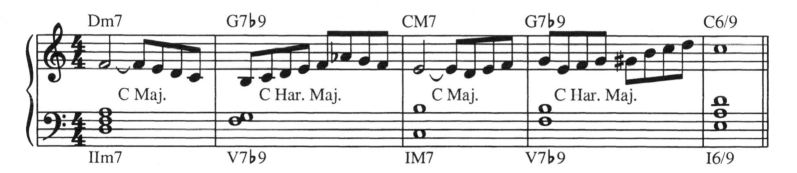

The harmonic major scale will complement the following chord types:

Dom. 7 ♭9

Dom. 7 ♭9 ♯9(♯5)

Dim.

The harmonic major scales in all keys appear at the conclusion of the chapter. The chords which complement each scale are written underneath.

This chapter discusses more complicated chord/scale relationships. For best results do not play the scale from root to root.

The harmonic major scale complements the V7♭9 in major keys. Play the scale which has the same letter name as the I chord. This scale is an especially good choice when only the ♭9 is to be emphasized in the V7 chord.

When the VI7♭9 chord progresses to the IIm7, the harmonic minor scale is preferred (see Chapter 4). A very common chord progression is IIIm7 (treated as a I chord - see Chapter 2) -VI7♭9-IIm7-V7♭9. The two ♭9 chords are treated differently because of their function. The VI7♭9 takes the harmonic MINOR scale while the V7♭9 takes the harmonic MAJOR scale. The VI7♭9 chord/scale contains the ♯5.

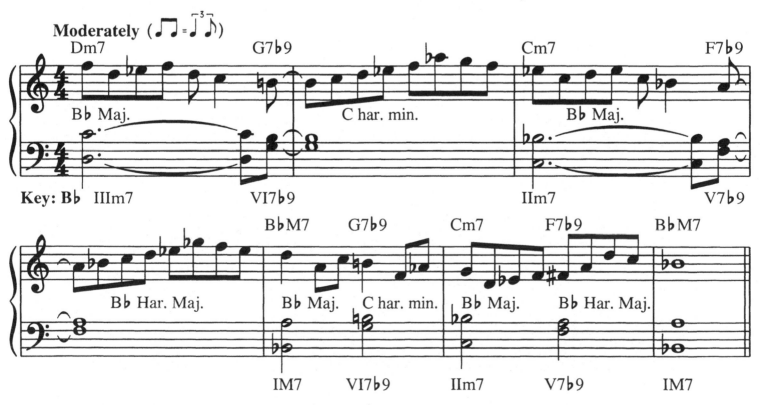

Below is a very common melodic idea based upon the previous example.

The ♭9 and ♯9 along with the ♯5 may be emphasized with the harmonic major scale. This use of the scale works best in minor keys with the V7 chord. Play the harmonic major scale whose tonic is a major third below the root of the V7 chord. (Ex. G7♭9(♯9) play E♭ harmonic major.)

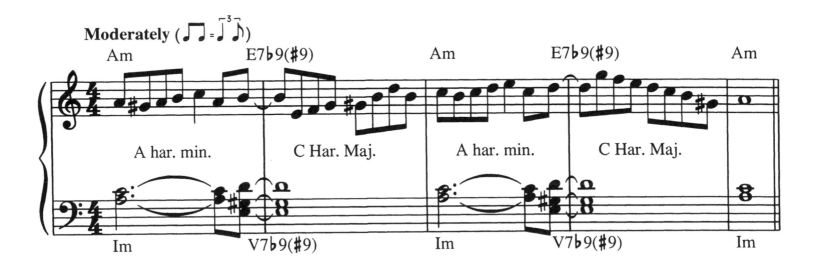

This scale works well with diminished seventh chords. When the I chord is diminished, play the harmonic major scale whose tonic is a perfect 5th above the chord root. Do not play this scale from tonic to tonic. (Ex. Cdim. play G harmonic major.)

Do not emphasize the tonic with this chord/scale relationship. The example below does not contain the tonic (C).

The next two examples include the Idim in a typical chord progression.

When the diminished seventh functions as a ♯I or a ♯II the chord/scale relationship changes. Both situations take the harmonic major scale whose tonic as a major 3rd above the chord root. (Ex: Cdim play E harmonic major) Reminder: Do not play the scale from tonic to tonic.

The next two examples illustrate a common jazz chord progression with diminished seventh chords.

The next example is the same chord progression but the chords change every two beats. Notice how the scales are linked together.

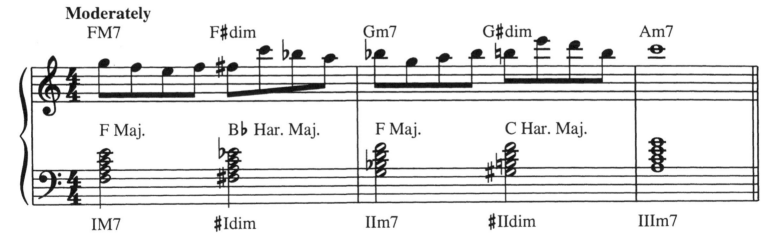

SUMMARY

Chord	Function	Harmonic Major Scale
C7♭9	V7 Maj. key	F
C7♭9(♯9)(♯5)	V7 min. key	A♭
Cdim	I	G
Cdim	♯I	E
Cdim	♯II	E

An eight measure improvisation follows which illustrates two uses of the harmonic major scale. As with all examples, this improvisation over-uses scales. A better improvisation would include scale tones mixed with chord tones, pentatonic and blues scales.

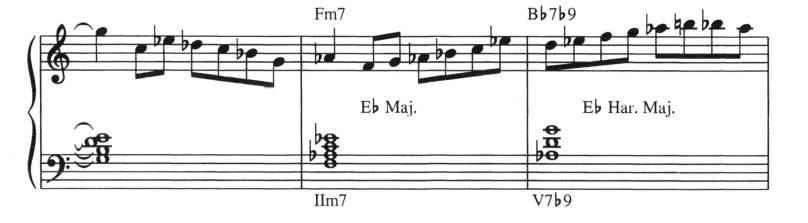

HARMONIC MAJOR SCALES

33

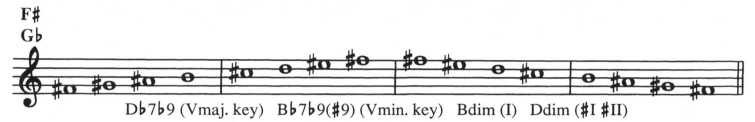

F#
Gb

Db7b9 (Vmaj. key) Bb7b9(#9) (Vmin. key) Bdim (I) Ddim (#I #II)

G

D7b9 (Vmaj. key) B7b9(#9) (Vmin. key) Cdim (I) Ebdim (#I #II)

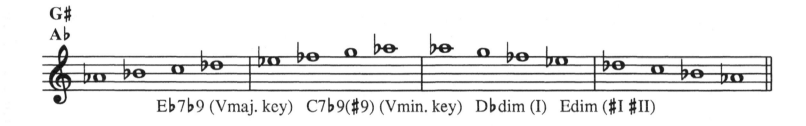

G#
Ab

Eb7b9 (Vmaj. key) C7b9(#9) (Vmin. key) Dbdim (I) Edim (#I #II)

A

E7b9 (Vmaj. key) Db7b9(#9) (Vmin. key) Ddim (I) Fdim (#I #II)

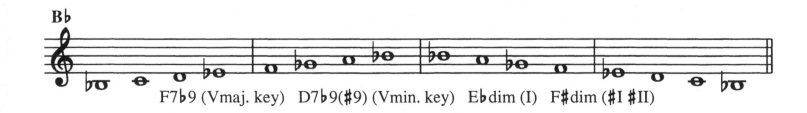

Bb

F7b9 (Vmaj. key) D7b9(#9) (Vmin. key) Ebdim (I) F#dim (#I #II)

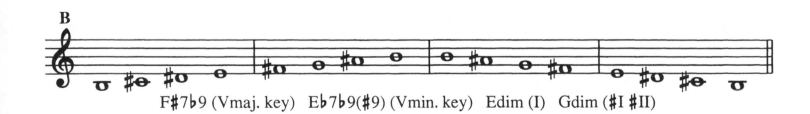

B

F#7b9 (Vmaj. key) Eb7b9(#9) (Vmin. key) Edim (I) Gdim (#I #II)

6: THE MELODIC MINOR SCALE

Unlike the classical melodic minor scale, the jazz version is the same ascending and descending.

The Jazz Melodic Minor Scale:

The melodic minor scale will complement the following chord types:

> m6
> m(maj7)
> dom. 7th ♯5
> dom. 7th ♯11
> dom. 7th ♯5 ♭9 ♯9 ♯11
> m7♭5(♯9)

The melodic minor scales in all keys appear at the end of this chapter. The chords which complement each scale are written underneath.

The melodic minor scale which has the same letter name as the chord root will complement the m6 and m(maj7) chords regardless of function. This is an especially good scale for the I chord in minor keys.

Emphasizing the 6th:

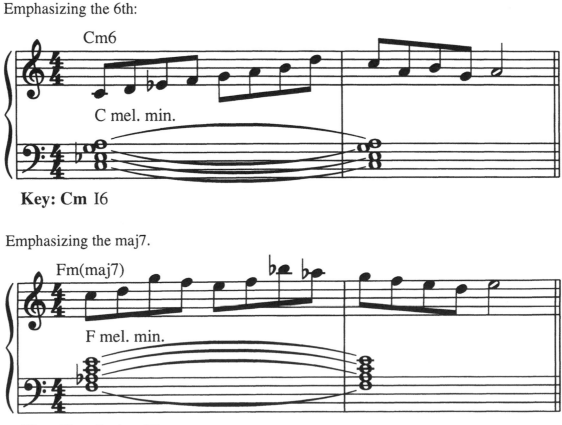

Key: Cm I6

Emphasizing the maj7.

Key: Fm Im(maj7)

To emphasize the ♯5 in a dominant 7th chord, treat the chord as a V7 and play the melodic minor scale which has the same letter name as the I chord. Major keys only.

The ♯11 may be emphasized in a dominant 7th chord. Play the melodic minor scale whose tonic is a perfect 5th above the chord root. (Ex. C7♯11 play G mel. min.)

The IV7 chord in a major key may contain the ♯11.

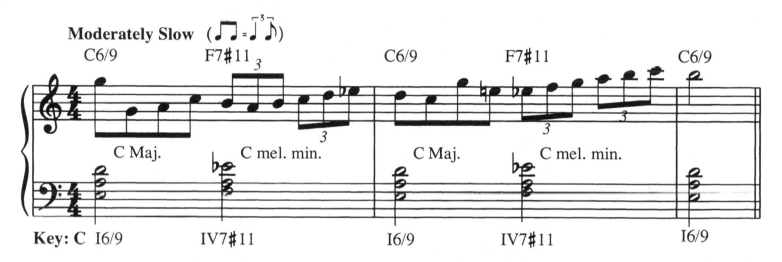

Very often the dominant 7th chord whose root is one half step above the I chord replaces the V7 chord in a major key. The ♯11 works well in this situation. The chord progression is IIm7-♭II7♯11-IM7 instead of the usual IIm7-V7-IM7.

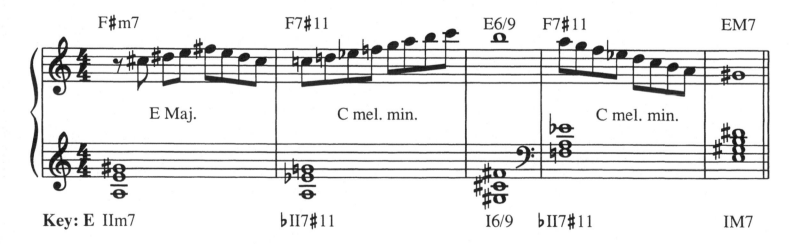

The preceding chord progression in several keys:

Key: G IIm7   ♭II7#11   IM7   **Key: F** IIm7

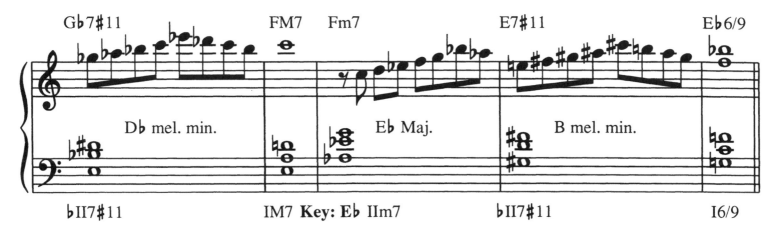

♭II7#11   IM7   **Key: E♭** IIm7   ♭II7#11   I6/9

This replacement device or substitution (as it is more often called) is also possible in minor keys. The chord progression is IIm7♭5-♭II7#11-Im6. The ♭II SUBSTITUTES for the V7 chord.

Fast

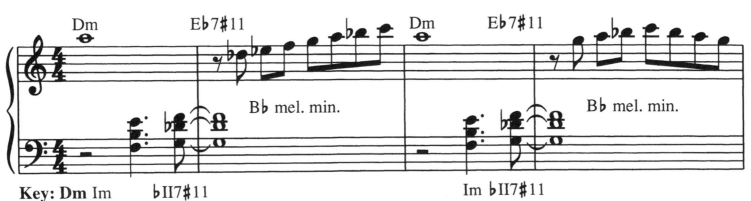

Key: Dm Im   ♭II7#11   Im ♭II7#11

Im   ♭II7#11   Im

The IV chord in a major key is sometimes m6.

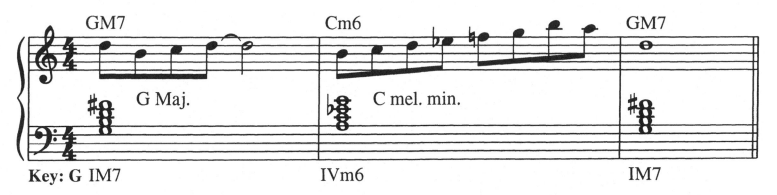

Key: G IM7   IVm6   IM7

A dominant 7th chord whose root is a perfect 4th above the IVm often substitutes for the IV minor chord. The ♯11 is added.

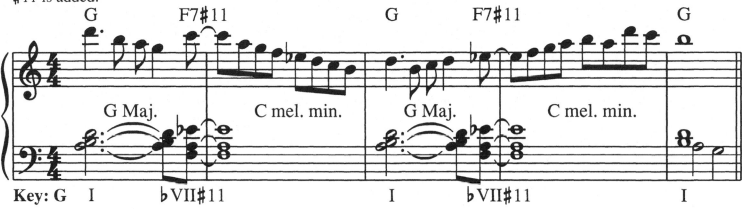

Key: G   I   ♭VII♯11   I   ♭VII♯11   I

The next example is a series of dominant 7th ♯11 chords.

The melodic minor scale may emphasize the ♯5 ♭9 ♯9 ♯11 in a dominant 7th chord. Play the scale whose tonic is a half step above the chord root. Usually the chord functions as a V7 in a major or minor key.

MAJOR KEY:

Key: F IIm7   V7alt.   I

MINOR KEY:

Sometimes the ♯9 is added to the m7♭5 chord. Play the melodic minor scale whose tonic is a minor 3rd above the chord root. This chord most often functions as a II chord in a minor key. (Ex. Cm7♭5♯9 play E♭ mel. min.)

The II7 chord in a minor key is treated as a temporary V7 in a minor key and takes the harmonic minor scale of the I chord.

THE III AND VI CHORDS IN MINOR KEYS

The next example illustrates a common chord progression with the III7 and VIM7 chords in a minor key. The III7 (F7) in measure four is preceded by a Cm7 chord and a temporary II-V in the key of B♭ is established. The next chord in measure five is a VIM7 (B♭M7). Ordinarily the B♭ major scale would seem correct for this chord as it is preceded by a II-V. This chord is treated as a VI chord in a minor key because it is followed by the V7 chord and is complemented by the minor scale which has the same letter name as the I chord.

In summary, in a minor key the III7 chord is treated like any dominant 7th chord. The VI major seventh chord takes the scale of the I chord.

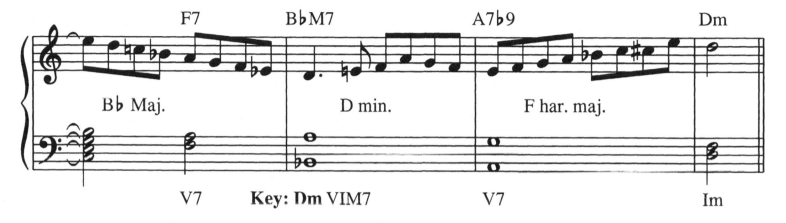

In the next minor key example, the VI chord is a dominant seventh. Play the melodic minor scale whose tonic is a perfect 5th above the chord root.

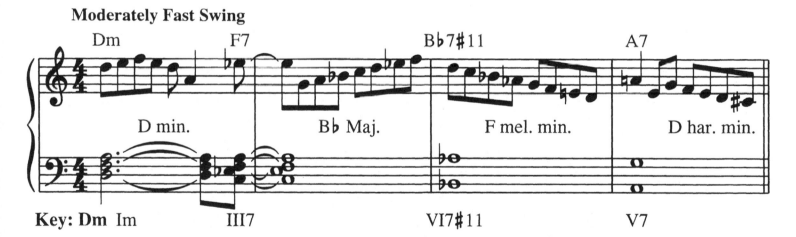

SUMMARY

Chord	Function	Melodic Minor Scale
Cm6	any	C
Cm(maj7)	any	C
C7#5	V major key	F
C7#11	any	G
C7#5(♭9)(#9)(#11)	V major minor keys	D♭
Cm7♭5(#9)	any	E♭

The following example applies most of the scales presented thus far to a typical chord progression.

MELODIC MINOR SCALES

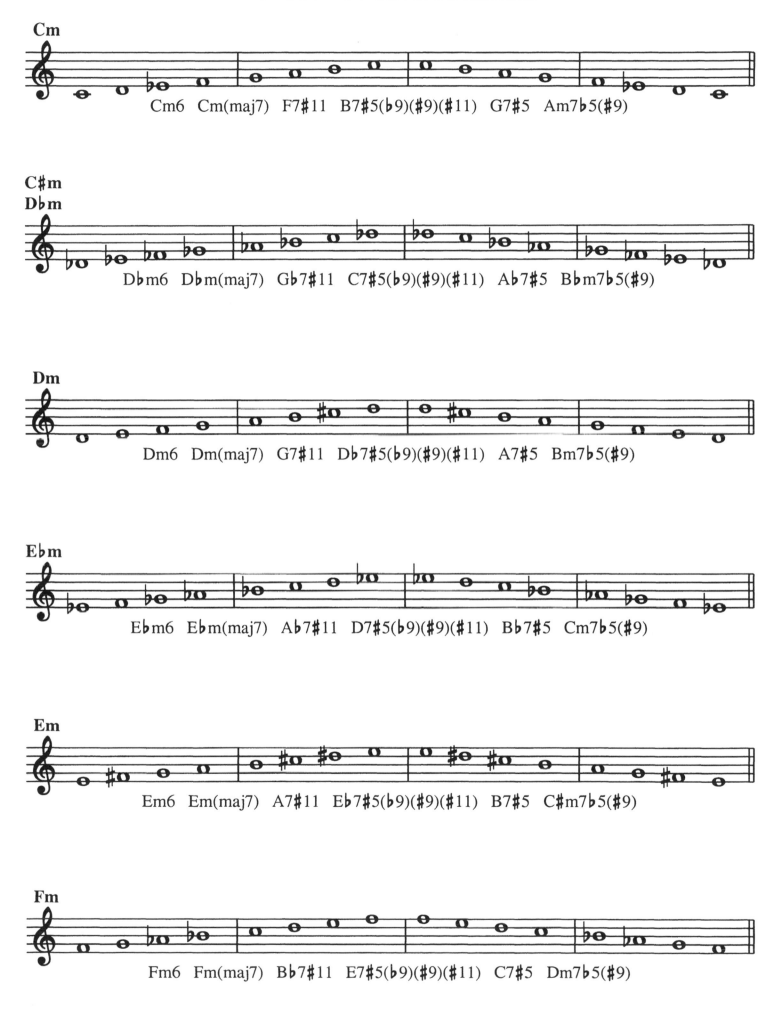

F#m
Gbm

Gbm6 Gbm(maj7) B7#11 F7#5(b9)(#9)(#11) Db7#5 Ebm7b5(#9)

Gm

Gm6 Gm(maj7) C7#11 Gb7#5(b9)(#9)(#11) D7#5 Em7b5(#9)

G#m
Abm

Abm6 Abm(maj7) Db7#11 G7#5(b9)(#9)(#11) Eb7#5 Fm7b5(#9)

Am

Am6 Am(maj7) D7#11 Ab7#5(b9)(#9)(#11) E7#5 F#m7b5(#9)

Bbm

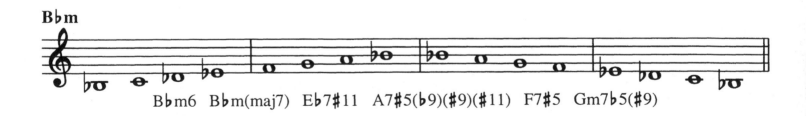

Bbm6 Bbm(maj7) Eb7#11 A7#5(b9)(#9)(#11) F7#5 Gm7b5(#9)

Bm

Bm6 Bm(maj7) E7#11 Bb7#5(b9)(#9)(#11) F#7#5 Abm7b5(#9)

7: THE DIMINISHED SCALE

There are two diminshed scales which share the same tonic. The first begins with a whole step followed by a half step followed by a whole step etc.... The abbreviation is W/H.

C Diminished Scale W/H:

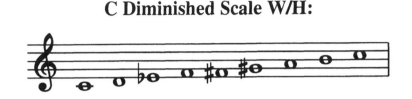

Chords: Dim. 7th

The second diminished scale begins with a half step followed by a whole step and continues half step/whole step. The abbreviation is H/W.

C Diminished Scale H/W:

Chords: Dom. 7th ♭9 ♯9 ♯11

The two diminished scales in all keys appear at the end of this chapter. The chords for each scale are written underneath.

The W/H diminished scale is played with dim. 7th chords regardless of function. Select the scale which has the same letter name as the chord root.

44

Sequential patterns work well with this scale.

A common chord progression on the diminished 7th chords:

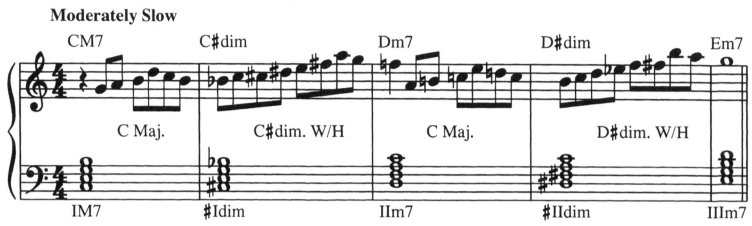

The diminished W/H scale as a fill-in:

The H/W diminished scale emphasizes the ♭9 ♯9 ♯11 in a dominant 7th chord. Select the scale which has the same letter name as the chord root.

This scale works well with the II-V-I progression in major keys.

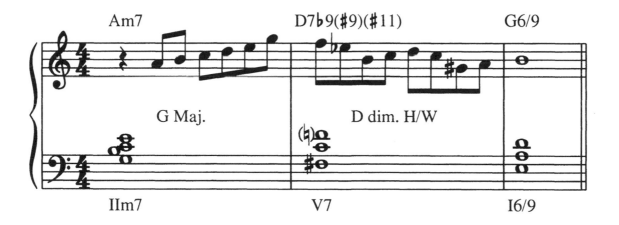

The diminished H/W scale with the ♭II7 chord substituting for the V7 chord:

The next example is a progression of dominant 7th chords.

The m7♭5(♯9) chord is sometimes combined with the V7 chord in a major key.

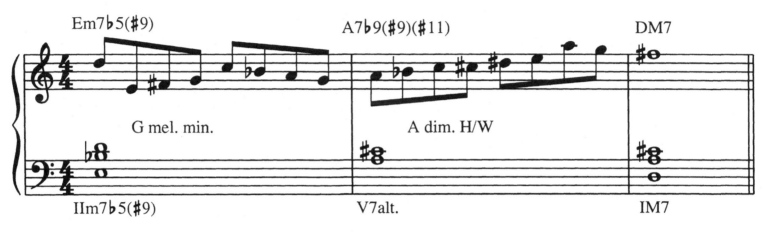

The half/whole diminished scale may be applied to a V7 chord leading to a I chord in a minor key.

SUMMARY

Chord	Function	W/H dim. Scale	H/W dim. Scale
Cdim	any	C	
C7♭9(♯9)(♯11)	any		C

DIMINISHED SCALES (WHOLE/HALF)

48

F#
Gb

F#dim

G

Gdim

G#
Ab

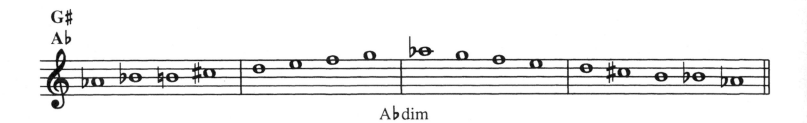

Abdim

A

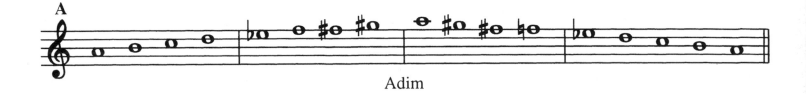

Adim

Bb

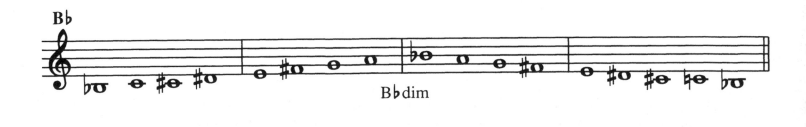

Bbdim

B

Bdim

DIMINISHED SCALES (HALF/WHOLE)

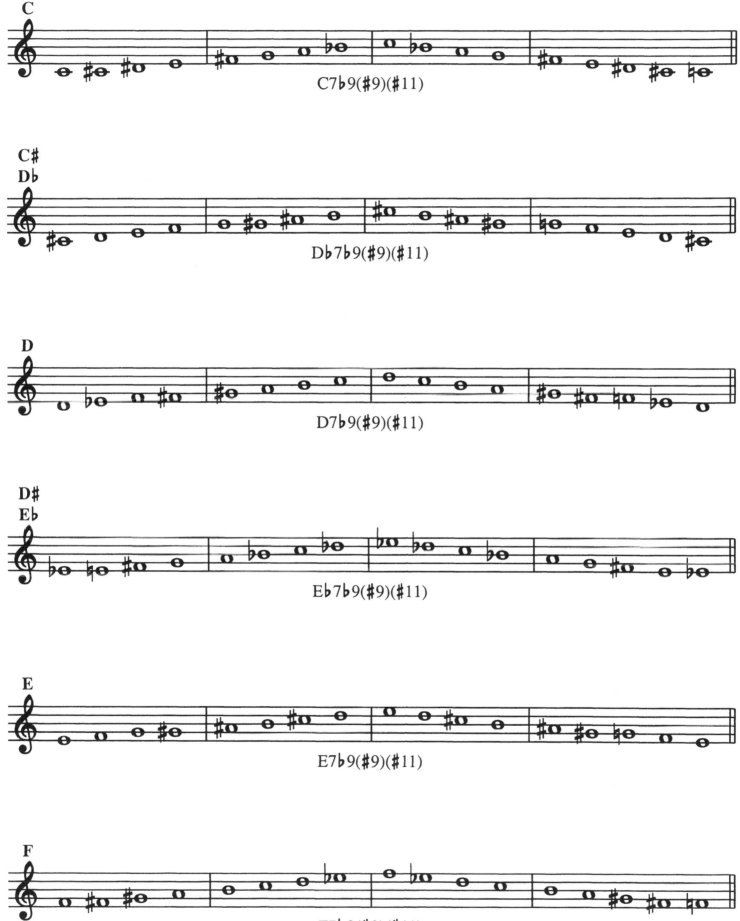

F#
Gb

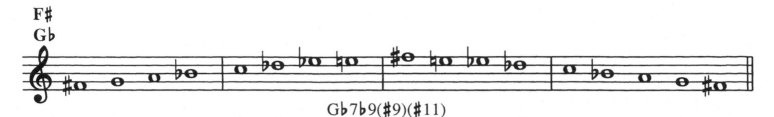

Gb7b9(#9)(#11)

G

G7b9(#9)(#11)

G#
Ab

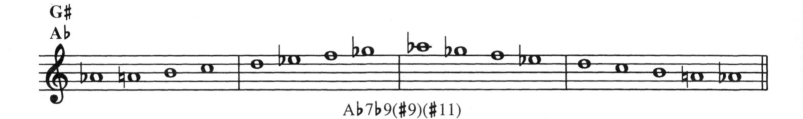

Ab7b9(#9)(#11)

A

A7b9(#9)(#11)

Bb

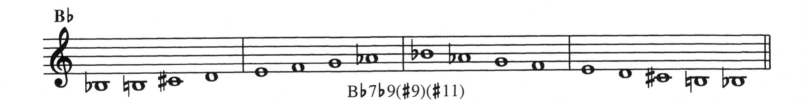

Bb7b9(#9)(#11)

B

B7b9(#9)(#11)

8: THE WHOLE TONE SCALE

C Whole Tone Scale:

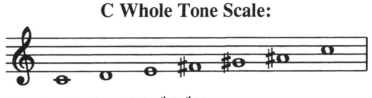

Chords: Dominant 7th #5 #11

The whole tone scales in all keys appear at the end of this chapter. The chords are written underneath.

The whole tone scale will emphasize the #5 and #11 in a dominant 7th chord. Play the scale which has the same letter name as the chord root.

In the following example the whole tone scale complements the V7 chord in the key of F major.

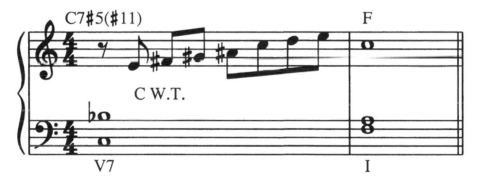

Sequential patterns are effective:

SUMMARY

Chord	Function	Whole Tone Scale
C7#5(#11)	any	C

WHOLE TONE SCALES

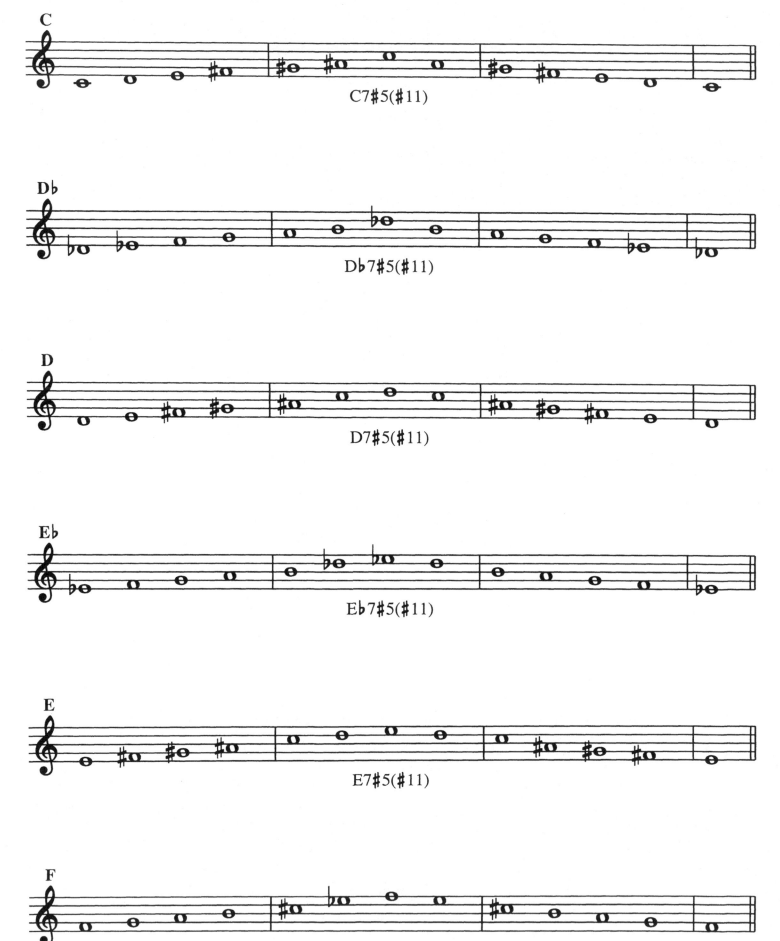

C

C7#5(#11)

Db

Db7#5(#11)

D

D7#5(#11)

Eb

Eb7#5(#11)

E

E7#5(#11)

F

F7#5(#11)

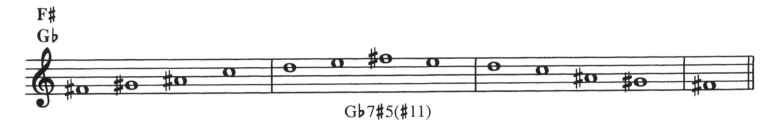

Gb7#5(#11)

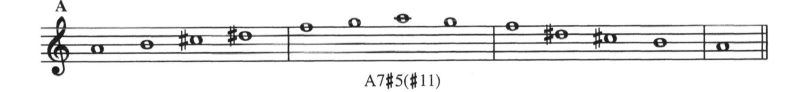

G7#5(#11)

Ab7#5(#11)

A7#5(#11)

Bb7#5(#11)

B7#5(#11)

CHORD/SCALE RELATIONSHIP CHART

To find the scale which complements any chord, transpose the following chart.

Chord	Function	Maj.	Min.	Har. Min.	Har. Maj.	Mel. Min.	Diminished	Whole Tone
C6/9	any	C						
CM7	I	C						
CM7	IV	G						
CM7	VI min. key	.	E					
CM7♯11	any	G						
Cm	I		C	C				
Cm6	I					C		
Cm6	IV		G			C		
Cm(maj7)	any				C	C		
Cm7 9 11	II	B♭						
Cm7	III	A♭						
Cm7	VI	E♭						
Cm7♭5	any		B♭					
Cm7♭5♯9	any					E♭		
C7 9 13	any	F						
C7♯5	V7 maj. key					F		
C7♭9	V7 maj. key				F			
C7♯11	any					G		
C7♯5♭9	any			F				
C7♯5(♯11)	any							C
C7♯5(♭9)(♯9)	V		F					
C7♯5(♭9)(♯9)	V min. key				A♭			
C7♭9(♯9)(♯11)	any						C h/w	
C7♯5(♭9)(♯9)(♯11)	any					D♭		
C7sus	V	B♭ no 4th						
Cdim	I				G		C w/h	
Cdim	♯I				E		C w/h	
Cdim	♯II				E		C w/h	

9: CHORDS

The chord tones may provide the basis for improvisations and fill-ins. The chord tones may be practiced in the traditional way.

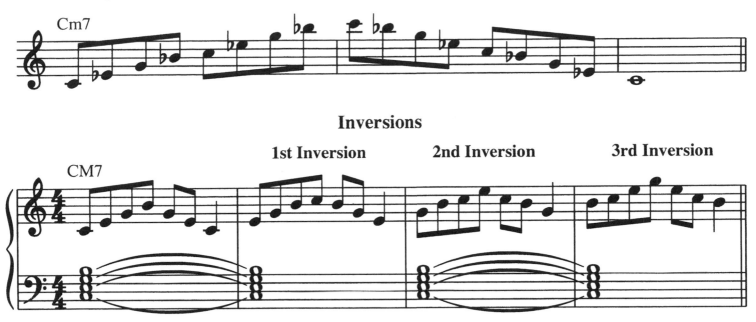

Inversions

The Cm6 is also the Am7♭5 chord.

The next two examples are melodies with chord tone fill-ins.

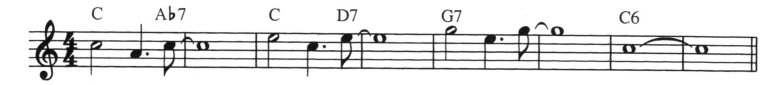

A more contemporary sound results when the chord tones are practiced in the following manner:

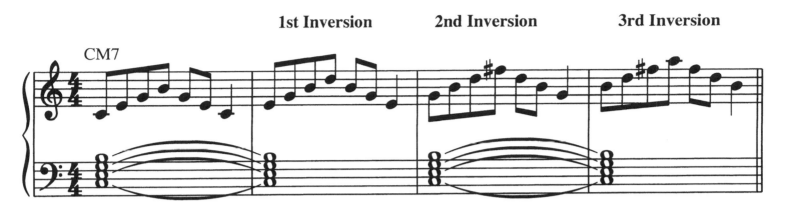

The top note of the diminished 7th chord is replaced by the note one whole step above. A more contemporary sound results.

58

The following examples are variations on the preceding exercises. Play the same left hand part.

Another variation:

The note which is one half step below each chord tone may be added. These notes are circled in the examples below.

Another variation:

The CHORD tones are circled in the following examples:

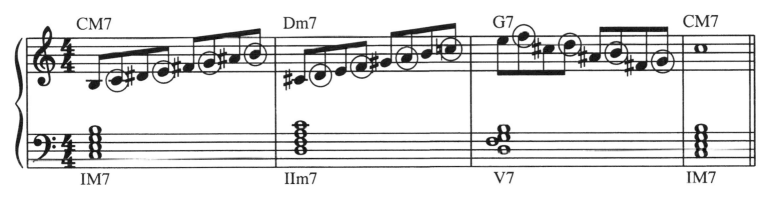

The note which is one SCALE step above the chord tone may be added.

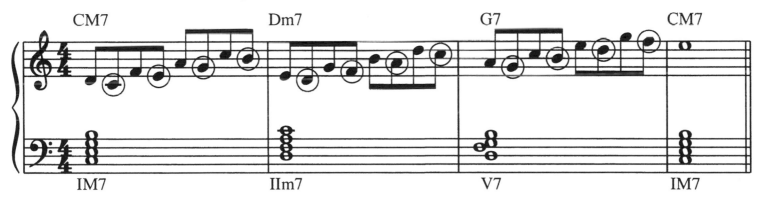

The next example adds the note one scale step above the chord tone and the note one half step below the chord tone. The chord tones are circled.

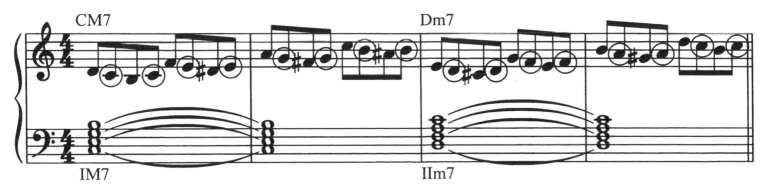

The two added notes may be played before the chord tones.

The next group of exercises link chord tones together in standard chord progressions. Both traditional and contemporary inversions appear.

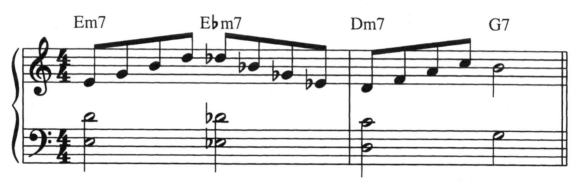

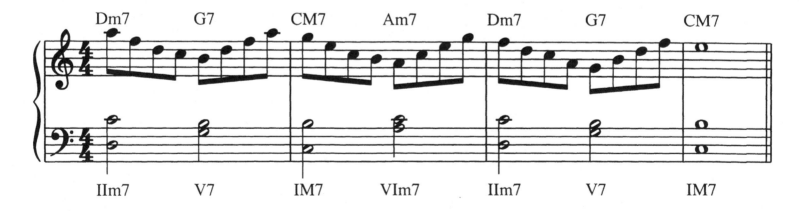

The chord tones may be played in any order.

The notes which are a half step below the chord tones are added and circled.

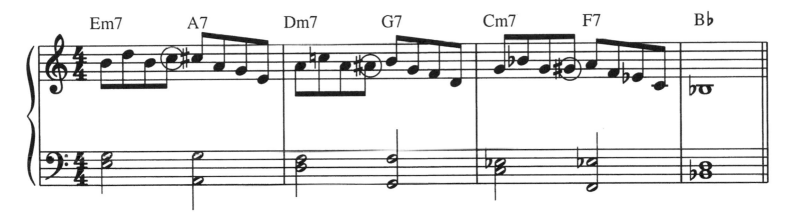

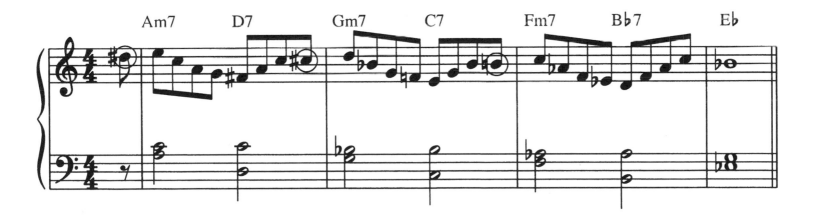

The chord tones may be played as arpeggios for endings, fill-ins and introductions. The next two examples are endings in the key of F major. In the first example the first inversion of the FM7 chord appears. All examples use the contemporary form of the inversion. (Page 57)

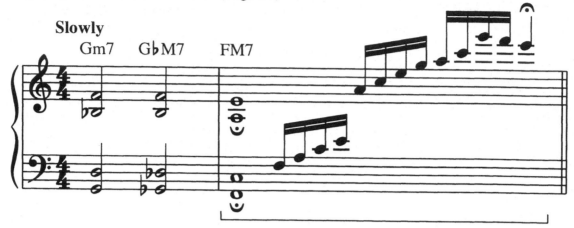

The FM7♯11 is played in second inversion.

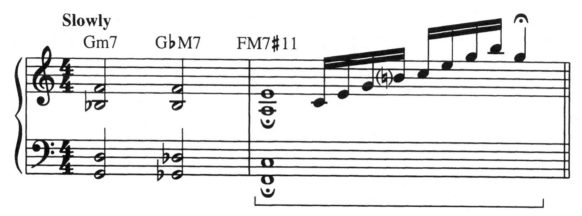

The next two examples illustrate arpeggios as fill-ins. The G7♯11 is played in third inversion.

The Gm11 is played in second inversion.

The first inversion of the C7 chord is played for an introduction.

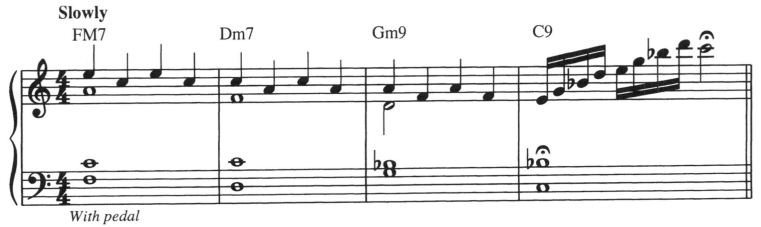

The following improvisation uses chord tones.

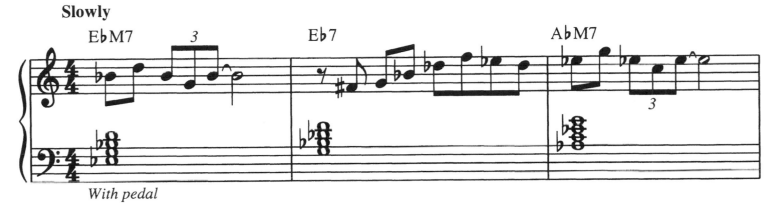

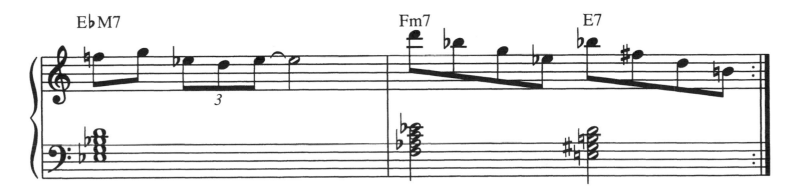

The above improvisation may sound somewhat contrived and uninteresting. The exclusive use of chord tones causes this effect. A good jazz improvisation also includes the traditional major and minor scales, pentatonic and blues scales. It is the skillful application of all the improvisational melodic devices which produces a good jazz line.

10: ALTERED DOMINANT 7TH CHORDS

One chord is superimposed upon the other in order to achieve the altered chord sound. In the example below the left hand plays C7 and the right hand plays D7. The resulting chord is C7#11.

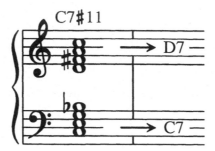

Five chords may be superimposed or played over a dominant 7th chord. The D7 Eb7 Gb7 Ab7 or A7 may be played over a C7 chord. The chart at the end of this chapter lists all superimposed chords for dominant seventh chords in all keys.

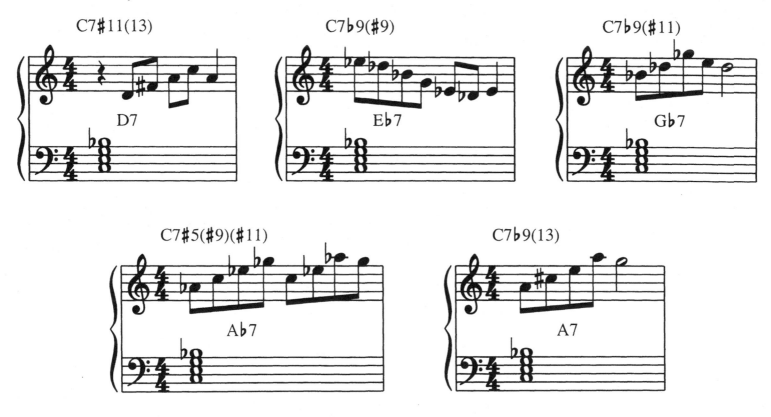

The diminished 7th chord whose root is the same letter name as the 7th in the dominant 7th chord is played over a dominant 7th chord. (Ex. C7 play Bb dim.)

For suspended chords play the m7 chord whose root is a perfect 5th above the chord root. (Ex. C7 play Gm7)
Only play root position or the 1st and 2nd contemporary inversion.

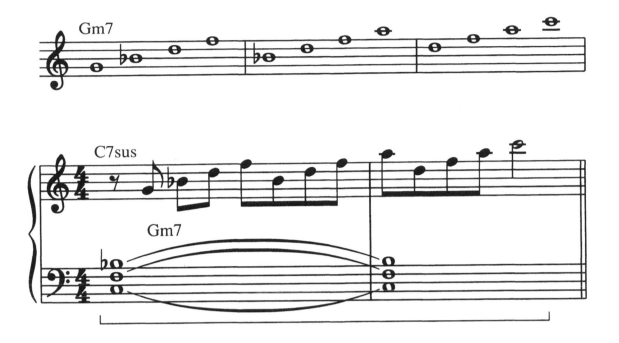

The contemporary diminished 7th chord may also be superimposed upon the dominant 7th chord.

Chord tones may be combined with the superimposed chords.

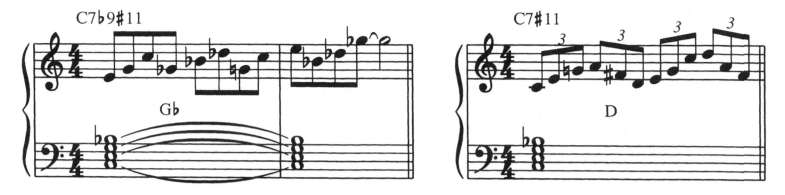

A typical chord progression with the diminished 7th chord superimposed upon the dominant 7th follows:

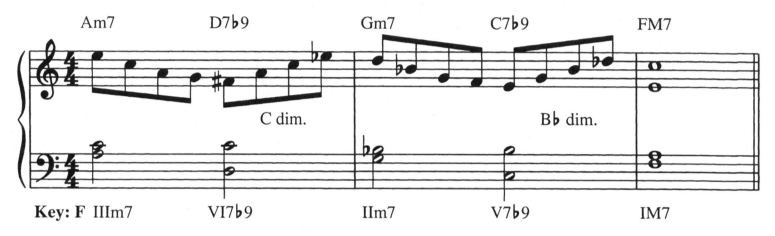

The contemporary diminished 7th chord played above the V7 chord:

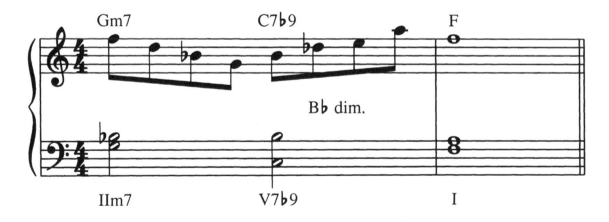

II-V-I in the key of C minor:

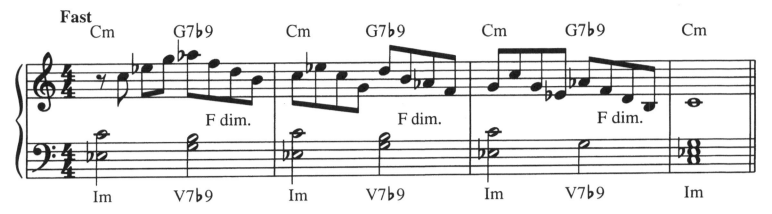

An introduction in the key of F major:

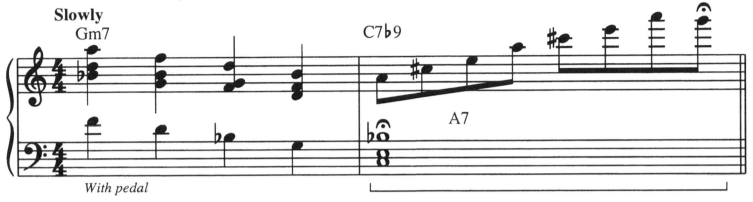

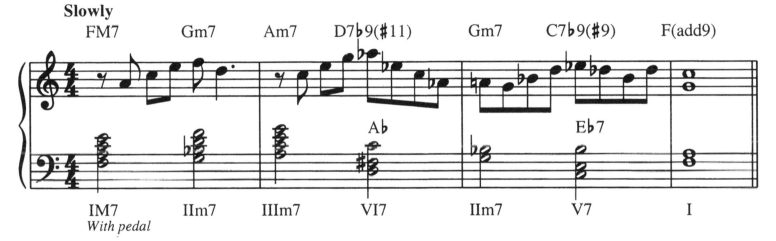

There are many "arpeggio-like" note combinations which may be superimposed upon several chord types. The following note pattern is most comfortable starting on the white keys.

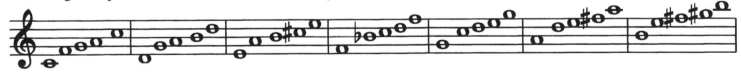

Each note pattern will complement seven different chords. Play the right hand with each of the left hand chords in the example below.

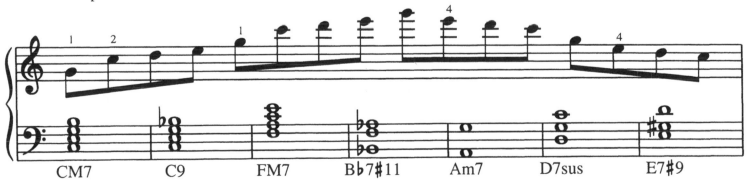

The next example illustrates this note pattern as an ending in the keys of C and F major.

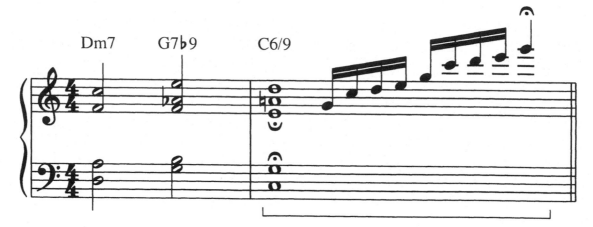

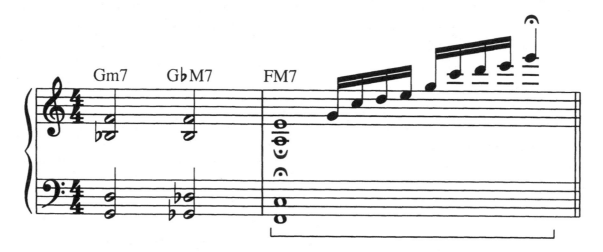

Two more ideas in C major and A minor:

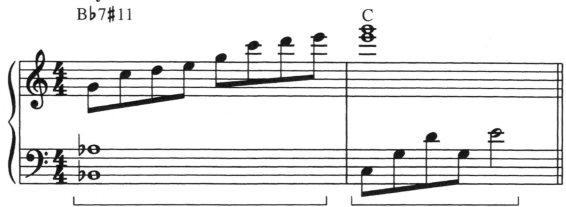

An ending with the V7sus chord:

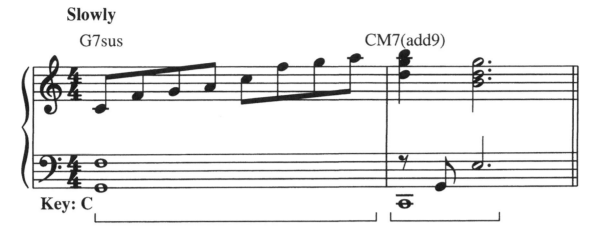

The next note pattern is the minor form of the first pattern.

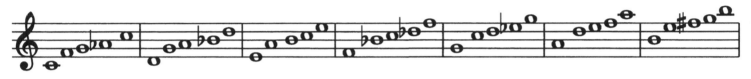

Play the right hand with each chord in the left hand.

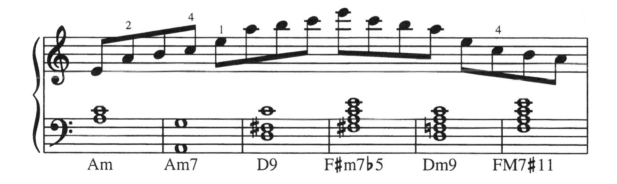

This pattern works well when the FM7♯11 functions as a IV chord.

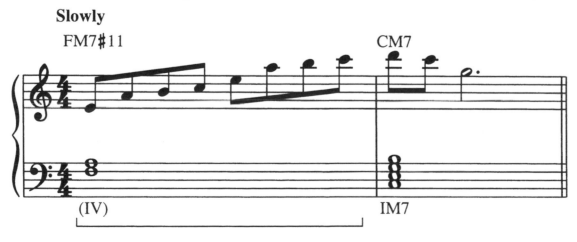

This note pattern is played with the II and I chords in the key of E minor.

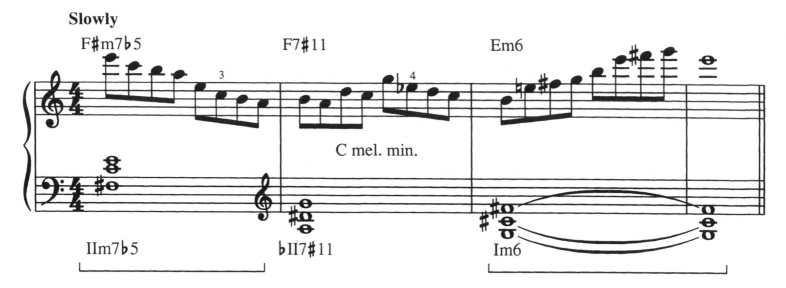

The next note pattern is based upon 4th intervals.

Each of the above patterns may be superimposed on FOURTEEN different chords! Play the right hand with each of the chords in the following example:

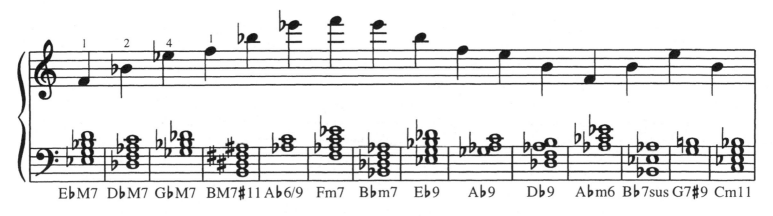

This note pattern is most effective as an arpeggio-like fill-in descending or ascending.

SUMMARY

SUPERIMPOSED CHORD CHART

Chord	#11	♭9#9	♭9#11	#5#9#11	♭9	♭9	sus
C7	D7	E♭7	G♭7	A♭7	A7	B♭dim	Gm7
D♭7	E♭7	E7	G7	A7	B♭7	Bdim	A♭m7
D7	E7	F7	A♭7	B♭7	B7	Cdim	Am7
E♭7	F7	G♭7	A7	B7	C7	D♭dim	B♭m7
E7	F#7	G7	B♭7	C7	C#7	Ddim	Bm7
F7	G7	A♭7	B7	D♭7	D7	E♭dim	Cm7
G♭7	A♭7	A7	C7	D7	E♭7	Edim	D♭m7
G7	A7	B♭7	D♭7	E♭7	E7	Fdim	Dm7
A♭7	B♭7	B7	D7	E7	F7	G♭dim	E♭m7
A7	B7	C7	E♭7	F7	F#7	Gdim	Em7
B♭7	C7	D♭7	E7	G♭7	G7	A♭dim	Fm7
B7	C#7	D7	F7	G7	A♭7	Adim	F#m7

72

11: COMBINING SCALES AND CHORDS

Scales and chords may be combined within the phrase.

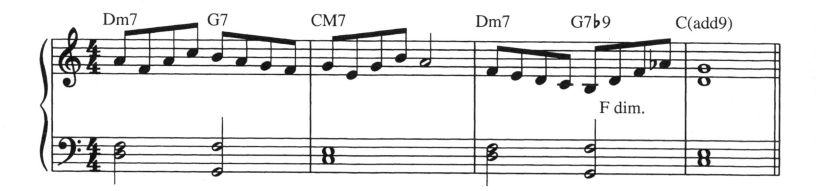

Sometimes only two or three notes of the chord or scale are present.

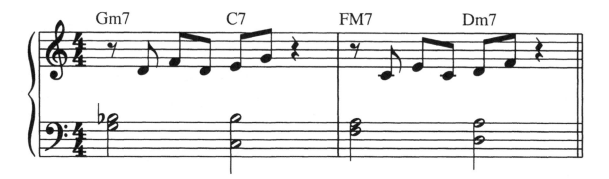

The following exercises provide examples of combining scales and chords. Notes which are a half step below the chord tones may appear.

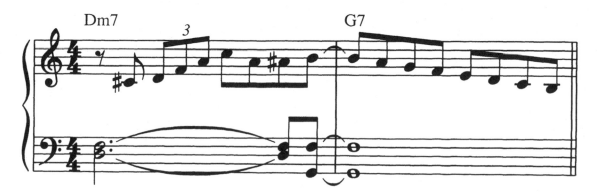

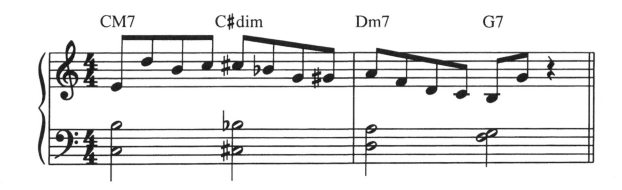

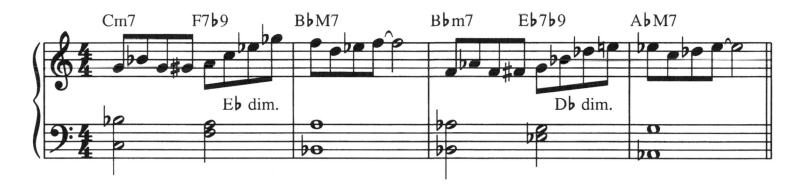

A variation on the above note pattern:

Key: Dm

In the next example notice how the original two measure improvisation is changed with different rhythm patterns. In practical playing situations all of the examples in this book could be enhanced by using more complicated rhythm patterns.

The note which is one half step above the chord tone may be added. These notes are marked with an arrow in the following examples:

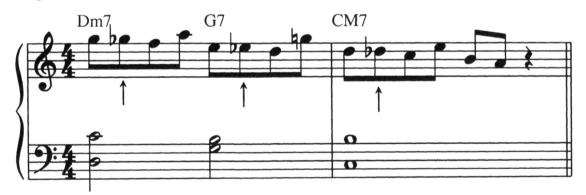

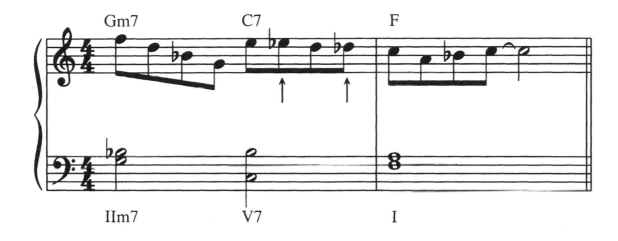

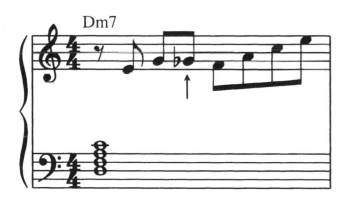

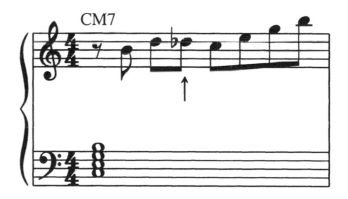

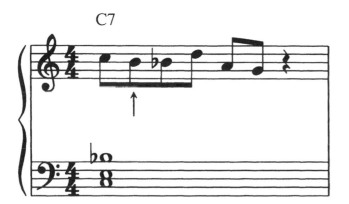

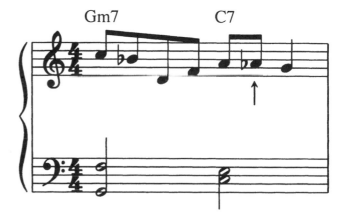

12: CODA

There are several devices such as grace notes, mordents and turns, which, when applied to the scales and chords, will enhance the improvisation. The discussion of these devices is covered in most books on jazz improvisation and is beyond the scope of this book.

No attempt has been made to include the so-called blues notes, pentatonic and blues scales. Information on these subjects is available in the author's books entitled EXPLORING JAZZ SCALES FOR KEYBOARD and EXPLORING BASIC BLUES FOR KEYBOARDS. Both are published by Hal Leonard.

It must be stressed once again that the scales and chords presented in this volume are not meant to be played exclusively for fill-ins or improvisations. The pentatonic and blues scales are also part of a good jazz line. It is the skillful combination of all the available melodic materials which produces a good jazz line.

The purpose of this book is to explore and to recognize the potential of scales and chords as applied to fill-ins, endings and improvisation. If the keyboard player is able to find a way to include some of these scales and chords in practical playing situations, the study of this book will have been worthwhile.

This chapter contains two improvisations. The first is a standard jazz chord progression and the second is the twelve measure blues. These improvisations will seem somewhat contrived because their purpose is to present the linking of scales and chords in a clear and simple manner. Each of the following improvisations is accompanied by a measure by measure analysis.

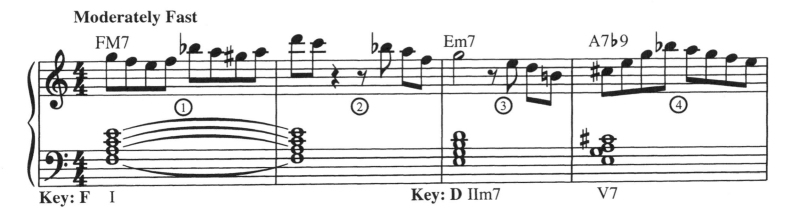

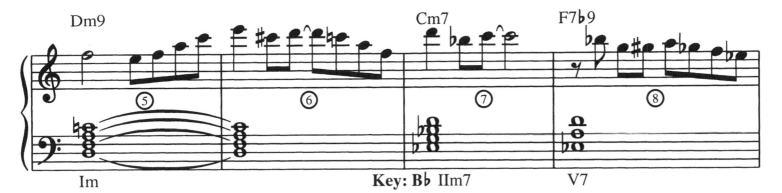

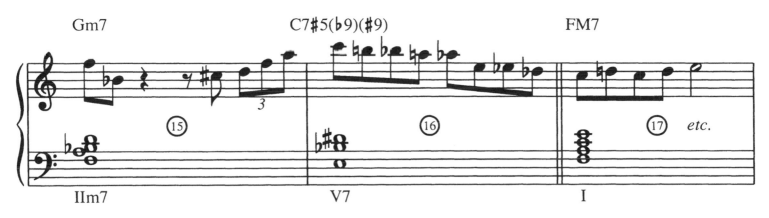

Analysis:

Measure		
1 - 2	Notes above and below F chord tones
3	Em7 chord tones
4	G dim. chord D har. min. scale
5	Dm7 chord tones
6	Dm7 chord C♯ is 1/2 step below chord tone
7	Cm7 chord tones
8	B♭ har. maj. scale G♯ is 1/2 step below chord tone
9	B♭ chord tones C♯ is 1/2 step below chord tone
10	B♭ mel. min. scale
11 - 12	FM7 chord tones
13	D mel. min. scale
14	D mel. min. scale G♭ is 1/2 step above chord tone
15	Gm7 chord tones C♯ is 1/2 step below chord tone
16	D♭ mel. min. scale B and A are 1/2 step above scale tones
17	F major scale

The following blues improvisation does not use the standard basic blues chord progression. Instead the chord progression reflects a later period in jazz.

Analysis:

Measure		
1	C maj. scale
2	A min. scale E7 chord tones
3	G maj. scale C dim. chord tones.
4	Gm7 chord tones B♭ dim. chord tones
5	F maj. scale (chord is temporary I function)
6	Fm7 chord E♭ scale
7	C chord tones F is 1/2 step above chord tone
8	D har. min. scale
9	Dm7 chord tones
10	G dim. scale H/W
11	C scale E♭ scale
12	A♭ scale A♭ mel. min. scale

Moderately Fast

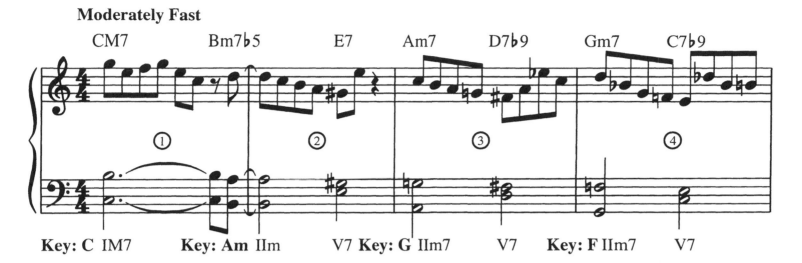

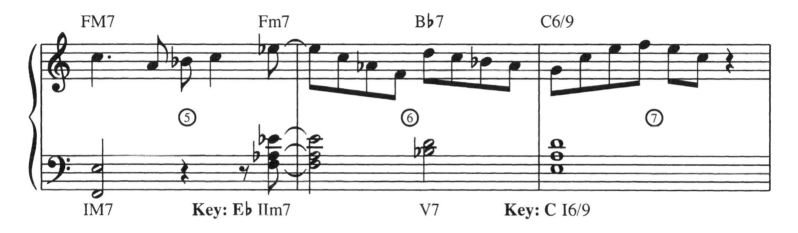

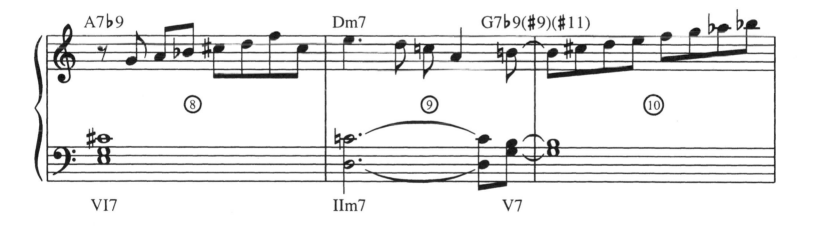

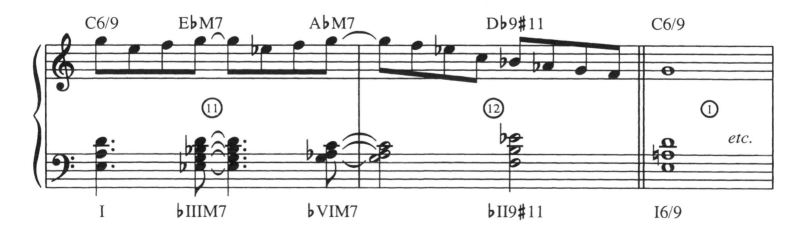

COMMON CHORD PROGRESSIONS
WITH CHORD/SCALE RELATIONSHIPS

C MAJOR

Chord Function Scale						
C I C Maj.	Am7 VIm7 C Maj.	Dm7 IIm7 C Maj.	G7 V7 C Maj.			
C I C Maj.	F IV C Maj.	C I C Maj.	Fm6 IVm6 C min. F mel. min.	C#11 I#11 G Maj.		
Em7 IIIm7 C Maj.	A7#5b9 VI7#5b9 D har. min.	Dm7 IIm7 C Maj.	G7b9 V7b9 C Har. Maj.	C6/9 I6/9 C Maj.	G7#5 V7#5 C mel. min. G W.T.	C I C Maj.
Dm7 IIm7 C Maj.	Db7#11 bII7#11 Ab mel. min.	Cmaj7 Imaj7 C Maj.	F7 IV7 C mel. min.	Cmaj7 Imaj7 C Maj.		
C6/9 I6/9 C Maj.	B7#5(b9) VII7#5(b9) E har. min.	E7#5(b9) III7#5(b9) A har. min.	A7#5(b9) VI7#5(b9) D har. min.	D7 II7 G	G7 alt. V7 alt. Ab mel. min. G H/W dim.	C6/9 I6/9 C Maj.
C I C Maj.	C#dim #Idim F Har. Maj. C#W/H dim.	Dm7 IIm7 C Maj.	D#dim #IIdim G Har. Maj. D#W/H dim.	Em7 IIIm7 C Maj.		

D MINOR

Chord Function Scale					
Em7b5 IIm7b5 D min.	A7#5(b9) V7#5(b9) D har. min.	Dm Im D min.			
Em7b5(#9) IIm7b5(#9) G mel. min.	A7 alt. V7 alt. F Har. Maj. Bb mel. min. A H/W dim.	Dm(maj7) Im(maj7) D mel. min.			
Em7b5 IIm7b5 D min.	Eb7#11 bII7#11 Bb mel. min.	Dm6 Im6 D mel. min.			
Dm Im D min.	F7 III7 Bb Maj.	Bbmaj7 VImaj7 D min.	A7 alt. V7 alt. D har. min.	Dm6 Im6 D mel. min.	
		Bb7 VI7 F mel. min.			